The Grapes of Wrath

John Steinbeck

Curriculum Unit

Rita M. Yeasted

The Center for Learning

Rita M. Yeasted earned her Ph.D. at Duquesne University. She has many years of experience teaching at the middle-school, secondary, and college levels.

The Publishing Team
Rose Schaffer, M.A., President/Chief Executive Officer
Bernadette Vetter, M.A., Vice President
Diane Podnar, M.S., Production Director
Amy Richards, M.A., Editor

Cover Design
Mary Souders

List of credits found on Acknowledgments page
beginning on 90.

ISBN-13: 978-1-56077-129-6
ISBN-10: 1-56077-129-1

Contents

Introduction

In April, 1939, Viking Press published what most critics regard as John Steinbeck's masterpiece, *The Grapes of Wrath*. Although the novel's earthy language shocked many readers, by May it had moved to the top of the best-seller list and was selling at the rate of nearly 10,000 copies a week. It became the top-selling book of 1939 and remained one of the ten best-sellers of 1940. Unlike many other American novels, *The Grapes of Wrath* has never gone out of print.

Critics have called it propaganda, sentimental, and obscene—but half a century later we are still moved by the story of the Joads and the thousands like them who lost their land in the midst of the Great Depression and the Dust Bowl of the mid-Thirties.

Like many American authors, Steinbeck was a journalist as well as a writer of fiction. He went into the fields with a photographer from *Life,* but would accept only travel expenses because "the suffering is too great for me to cash in on it."[1] When George West of the *San Francisco News* approached him in 1936 to write a series of articles on the agricultural conditions of the San Joaquin Valley, he immediately set out for the squatters' camp in the company of the director in charge of management of migrant-camp programs, Eric H. Thomsen. "I want to put a tag of shame on the greedy bastards who are responsible for this," he wrote, "but I can best do it through newspapers" (*Letters,* p. 162). The series contained poignant stories of individuals he met on his journey, but Steinbeck needed a larger outlet for the anger he felt over the conditions he experienced in his native California.

For two years he worked on a 60,000-word manuscript entitled "L'Affaire Lettuceberg," a biting satire that he decided to burn because it "would not help people to understand each other." He completed *The Grapes of Wrath* in six months. Banned and burned in cities across the country, the novel remains long after the names of its critics.

In an age of concern over the plight of America's farmlands, earth's fragile environment, and the growing problem of pollution, *The Grapes of Wrath* is still relevant. In an age when Third World peoples are the "new Okies," when people step over the sleeping homeless in our major cities, and the gap between rich and poor widens, *The Grapes of Wrath* is still relevant. The movement from "I" to "we," this novel's major theme, challenges every new generation of readers.

John Steinbeck, in a letter to his editor, Pascal Covici (1/16/39), wrote that there are five layers to this novel and that readers will find as many as they can and won't find any more than they have in themselves (*Letters,* pp. 178-9). Use of this curriculum unit will enable teacher and students to uncover the layers of this unforgettable American classic and, in the process, learn something of America.

---

[1]*Steinbeck: A Life in Letters,* ed. Elaine Steinbeck and Robert Wallsten (New York: Viking Press, 1975), 178–9. Referred to hereafter as *Letters*.

About the Author

John Ernest Steinbeck was born February 27, 1902, in Salinas, California. In 1925, he left Stanford University without a degree, went to New York City and worked as a construction laborer and reporter. He returned to California the following year and published *Cup of Gold* in 1929. In 1930 he married Carol Henning and first met marine biologist, Ed Ricketts, a colleague and friend whose work greatly influenced Steinbeck's philosophy. In 1933, *To a God Unknown* and the first two parts of *The Red Pony* were published. He won the O. Henry prize for "The Murder" in 1934.

Tortilla Flat brought him his first financial success and the Commonwealth Club of California Gold Medal in 1935. *In Dubious Battle,* published in 1936, was a forerunner of *The Grapes of Wrath.* In 1937 he published *Of Mice and Men* and moved to New York to work on the stage version, for which he won the Drama Critics' Circle Award for the season. Three parts of *The Red Pony* were published, he traveled to Europe, and late in 1937 he went west from Oklahoma with migrants. *The Grapes of Wrath* appeared in the spring of 1939. Steinbeck won the Pulitzer Prize for it in 1940.

His marine biology expeditions produced *Sea of Cortez* in 1941. The *Moon Is Down* was published in 1942. The war years brought divorce, remarriage to Gwyndolen Conger (Verdon), and several months as a war correspondent. *Cannery Row* appeared in 1945, along with the fourth chapter of *The Red Pony.* Two sons, Thomas and John, were born in 1944 and 1946. *The Pearl* and *The Wayward Bus* were published in 1947, the year he traveled to Russia. The following year he was elected to the American Academy of Arts and Letters and divorced from his second wife. Ed Ricketts died in a car-train collision that same year. Steinbeck married Elaine Scott in December, 1950, the year of *Burning Bright.*

Steinbeck's last works were *East of Eden* (1952), *Sweet Thursday* (1954), *The Short Reign of Pippin IV* (1957), *Once There Was a War* (1958), and *The Winter of Our Discontent* (1961). His last popular work, *Travels with Charley* (his dog), appeared in 1962, the year he became the sixth American to win the Nobel Prize for literature. He won the Press Medal of Freedom and the U.S. Medal of Freedom two years later. Steinbeck died on December 20, 1968, and was buried in his beloved Salinas.

Values:

- an appreciation for our common humanity
- the need to work together to achieve a common goal
- the need for compassion and justice for the oppressed
- the importance of avoiding stereotypes and labels
- the need to share what we have with others, especially the poor
- the importance of commitment to our beliefs
- a respect for our religious heritage and that of others
- the realization that change is part of the human condition
- the importance of caring about the earth and our environment
- an understanding of the role of technology in society

Teacher Notes

Because comprehending this long and complex novel requires a certain maturity, *The Grapes of Wrath* should probably be taught only to juniors or seniors, and is ideal for Advanced Placement classes. This unit provides sequential lessons involving individual and group work, class discussion questions, and ideas for enrichment. The exercises discuss style, structure, image patterns, characterization, philosophy, and history.

While some teachers may assign a quick reading of the novel before this unit is used, and this is highly recommended, a teacher may begin the novel with Lesson 1. The early lessons closely examine the first chapters of the book because a comprehension of the beginning of this novel will make reading the remaining chapters, if not easy, less difficult. The ending of the novel harks back to the beginning at so many levels that the careful reader should not be surprised at Rose of Sharon's action. Lessons 6-10 assume that the novel has been completed.

Teachers may choose any or all of the lessons and/or handouts in teaching this novel. The time devoted to each lesson is at the discretion of the teacher.

Audiovisual Resources

Steinbeck's Losers. Video transfer or filmstrip and tape. Thomas S. Klise Co., P.O. Box 317, Waterford, CT 06385.

Zanuck, Darryl (producer). *The Grapes of Wrath.* Director: John Ford, Screenplay by Nunnally Johnson. Starring Henry Fonda, Jane Darwell, John Carradine. 20th Century Fox, 1940. (128 mins.) Film. (Widely available in DVD and VHS format.)

Lesson 1
Getting into the Novel: Themes, Language, and Character

Objectives

- To introduce the novel, paying special attention to Steinbeck's use of color, sound, and image patterns

- To lay the groundwork for appreciation of the novel's themes and character development

- To begin exploration of the person/machine/animal relationships in the novel

Notes to the Teacher

Steinbeck's use of language is one of the noteworthy qualities of this novel. **Handouts 1–3**, covering the first four chapters of the novel, demand a close reading of the text. This lesson in close textual study will be valuable even if students have already read the novel—and will provide a methodology for the students to read other novels in the future.

Procedure

1. Introduce the novel by having a student or students read chapter one aloud. Distribute **Handout 1** and divide the class into small groups to answer the questions. You may decide to form groups which will remain together for the duration of the study of this novel.

   Suggested Answers

   1. *Sharp sun struck day after day; wheels mill the ground; horses' hooves beat the ground; sun flared; wind softly clashed drying corn; wind grew strong and hard; wind carried dust away; wind grew stronger; wind raced faster, dug cunningly among the rootlets of the corn; wind cried and whimpered over the fallen corn; sun was as red and ripe as new blood*

   2. *a) red, gray, pink, white, green, brown*
      b) bleached by the sun, becoming lifeless
   3. *Wind softly clashed the drying corn; wind cried and whimpered over the fallen corn; corn threshed the wind and made a dry, rushing sound; dust-filled air muffled sound more completely than fog does; roosters crowed and their voices were muffled*
   4. *their spirit*
   5. *Men's faces became hard and angry and resistant*

2. Assign chapters 2-4 in the novel. Distribute **Handout 2** to prepare for next class period. As a preparation for assignment, you may want to explain image patterns and symbols if terms are unfamiliar to students. For the purposes of studying this novel, simply define image patterns as sensory experiences captured in words, especially visual pictures. Symbols are any words, objects, actions, or characters that embody and evoke a range of additional meanings and significance.

3. In a second class period, use Handout 2 for discussion.

   Suggested Answers

   1. *a) truck and driver's face; b) Tom's cap and suit*
   2. *radio, truck's motor and tires*
   3. *a) Tom sees himself as a poor person who believes that other people like him would have more heart than the bosses.*
      b) Tom has a great deal of family pride, even though his folks are not highly educated.
      c) Tom essentially wants to avoid trouble.

1

4.   I.   II.
    flies   my dogs (feet)
                   "cat" (Caterpillar
    bees   tractor)
                   driver chewed like a
    grasshopper   cow
                   elephant's proboscis
                   whale's whanger
                   just done it for ducks
                   sling the bull
                   nose goin' over me
                       like a sheep in a
                       vegetable patch
    5. crushes it

4. If time permits, **Handout 3** may be used as a group project in class and then discussed. **Handouts 2** and **3** should help students with character analysis in this novel.

Suggested Answers

1. *The woman tries to avoid hitting it by swerving her car. The man tries to hit it by swerving his truck at it.*
2. *persevering, courageous, frantic*
3. *someone who plods along but arrives at a goal*
4. ***TURTLE***
   horny head
   hard legs
   yellow-nailed feet
   horny beak
   fierce, humorous eyes
   brows like fingernails

   JIM CASY
   long bony head, high forehead
   tight of skin
   set on a neck as stringy and muscular as a celery stalk
   eyeballs heavy and protruding
   lids stretched to cover them
   cheeks brown, shiny, hairless
   mouth full, humorous or sensual
   nose beaked and hard bare feet
5. *alike in their heads, feet, noses, general appearance*

Assignment: Read chapters 5–7.

Enrichment Exercise

If students are familiar with *Cry, the Beloved Country*, another way to introduce this novel could be to have one student read paragraph one of the first chapter of *The Grapes of Wrath* and another the first chapter of Paton's novel. The image patterns and use of color are remarkably similar. In each, the *land* is a major character in the novel.

Name _____

Date _____

The Land at War

1. In the first paragraph, Steinbeck describes the earth as "scarred," the ears of corn as "green bayonets," the weeds trying to "protect themselves." What other phrases describing the wind, sun, or dust indicate that the land is at war with harsh natural events?

2. a) Steinbeck uses colors in this chapter to paint a picture of Oklahoma during the drought of the 1930's. What colors does he choose?

   b) What does his progression of color (e.g., from red to pink) tell us about what is happening to the land?

3. Chapter 1 is filled with the sounds of nature. What descriptions of sound can you find in the chapter?

4. In the last paragraph of chapter 1, Steinbeck writes, "The women studied the men's faces secretly, for the corn could go, as long as something else remained." What do you think this "something else" is?

5. How can the women and children feel safe when the men do not know what to do?

How do they know "that there was no break"?

Name _____

Date _____

The Story Begins

1. a) The colors red and gray, which dominate chapter 1, play an important part in chapter 2 as well. The red sun is the "victor" in the natural world's war in chapter 1. What is colored red in chapter 2?

   b) The land "lost the war" to wind and sun in the first chapter, ending up a pale gray. What is colored gray in Steinbeck's second chapter?

2. The sounds of chapter 1 are of nature. In this chapter, where does the "music" come from?

3. Some of Tom Joad's first lines tell us a great deal about him. What do we learn of Tom from these lines?

   a) "Sure—I see [the No Riders sticker]. But sometimes a guy'll be a good guy even if some rich bastard makes him carry a sticker."

   b) "Well, I ain't heard [from my folks] lately. I never was no hand to write, nor my old man neither." He added quickly, "But the both of us can, if we want."

   c) "I don't mean nothin' neither," said Joad. "I'm just trying to get along without shovin' nobody around."

4. Throughout the novel, Steinbeck will tell of people, machines, and animals. Chapter 2 (like most) contains examples of all three: the red truck; the driver, Tom, and the waitress; and numerous examples of insect/animal life. List first the animal/insect life you find in this chapter, and in Column Two list the things which are compared to or called by animal names:

I

II

5. What does Tom do to the grasshopper?

Note: As you read this novel, note the way people treat the animals they encounter.

Name _____

Date _____

Tale of the Turtle

1. In chapter 3, a diversion from the Joad story, we again have the people/machine/animal triad. The turtle, carrying his house on his back, gets to the other side slowly but surely, but the two drivers react to the animal very differently. Explain.

2. Having read chapter 3 very carefully, list the adjectives you would use to describe this turtle in its journey to the other side of the road.

3. If a symbol is an action or thing that points beyond its concrete, literal meaning, what might the turtle symbolize?

4. List the words or phrases which describe the turtle and Jim Casy:

Turtle	Jim Casy

5. In the middle of chapter 4, Casy describes himself as being like the turtle, always going "off somewheres." In what ways do the turtle and the preacher resemble each other physically?

Lesson 2
Everything Connects: Examining the Novel's Parts

Objectives

- To introduce Steinbeck's use of intercalary chapters
- To continue the exploration of the people/machine/animal imagery
- To build a foundation for seeing the novel as a whole
- To develop a long-term reading project

Notes to the Teacher

Although Steinbeck once wrote of this novel, "It's just a book, interesting I hope, instructive in the same way the writing instructed me," he added, "Its structure is very carefully worked out. . . ."[1] Early critics of the novel did not agree with his 1955 comment, but no serious student of this novel can ignore the connecting links between the chapters. Sometimes an anonymous character echoes (or foretells) actions of one of the novel's main characters. Sometimes a small occurrence in one chapter is explored in depth in a succeeding chapter. In order to help students to see these links, **Handouts 4** and **5** provide exercises which show the relationships in these early chapters. Question 6 of **Handout 5** provides an opportunity to note the links in the remaining chapters of the book. **Handout 6** offers students a chance to keep a record of the numerous references to machines and animals in the novel. This will be used upon its completion with **Handout 24**.

Procedure

1. As a way of introducing intercalary chapters, show the relationship between chapters 1 and 2, as discussed in **Handout 2**, and between chapters 3 and 4, as discussed in **Handout 3**. Distribute **Handout 4** and allow students, who have now read chapter 5 of

the novel, to prepare answers through group work. Close class with discussion of their answers.

Suggested Answers: (Answers will vary.)

1. a) **Bank/Company**
   needs, wants, insists, must have had thought and feeling
   ensnared owners, cold and powerful masters
   don't breathe air, don't eat side-meat breathe profits
   eat interest on money
   has to have profits
   can't wait—will die without money keeps growing sick
   more than men who work there out of control
   can make men do what it wants

   b) **Owners**
   proud to be slaves
   owned cars
   told farmers to go West

   c) **Tractors**
   great crawlers
   move like insects
   strong as insects
   snub-nosed monsters with snouts

   d) **Man driving tractors**
   did not look like man
   gloved, goggled, rubber dust mask over nose and mouth
   part of the monster (a robot)
   perception muzzled
   speech muzzled
   protest muzzled
   could not see or smell land

2. *They are all concerned with profit and care little for the land or the people on it. They lack humanity.*
3. *$3 a day to feed his kids*
4. *"crushed like a bug"*
5. *Tom Joad crushes the grasshopper in his fingers in chapter 2.*

2. **Handout 5** allows you again to look closely at Steinbeck's use of language. You may wish to elicit various ways he uses language in the first five chapters. Chapter 7 allows you to provide

[1] As cited in Mary Ellen Caldwell, A New Consideration of the Intercalary Chapters in *The Grapes of Wrath*," in *Twentieth Century Interpretations of the Grapes of Wrath*, Ed. Robert Con Davis (Englewood Cliffs, N.J.: Prentice-Hall, 1982), 106.

comparisons of Steinbeck's style with other American writers. You may want to read aloud passages from Sandburg's *The People, Yes*, newsreel passages from John dos Passos' *USA*. (e.g., Newsreel 59, "The Stranger First Coming to Detroit"), or a passage from Whitman's "Song of Myself" (stanza 6 may be a good choice).

You may also want to use chapter 7 as a way of discussing characterization in the novel. The migrants' naivete can be contrasted with the salesmen's unscrupulousness. The handout may be begun in class and then kept for a long-term project. If you choose to use it, you may decide to distribute and explain **Handout 6** at this time.

Suggested Answers: (*Answers will vary.*)

1. *corner of house smashed in*
2. *Southwest*
3. *It makes the story more "human," keeps evil from being totally abstract.*
4. *It captures the fast-talking salesmen's speech.*
5. *Joads have made a bad deal on a Hudson 6 truck.*
6. *Because the links are many, there are numerous acceptable answers for this exercise. Here are some suggested responses:*
   Ch. 9 —*Joad family is preparing to leave in 8; junk dealers buy goods (lives) of Okies in 9.*
   10 — *Anonymous migrants sell goods at a loss in 9; Joads get only $18 for all their belongings in 10.*
   11 — *Joads pack up and leave their land in 10; the abandoned farms are described in 11.*
   12 — *Ch. 11 describes the country migrants leave; ch. 12 (another intercalary) begins the journey section of the novel and captures the nation in flight (Highway 66 chapter).*

13 — *Highway 66 (ch. 12) becomes the road the Joads travel (ch. 13).*
14 — *The changes in the lives of the Joads (ch. 13) reflect the changes and restlessness of the nation on the move (ch. 14). Wilsons join the Joads; Grampa dies. "Fambly" becoming extended family.*
15 — *Another Highway 66 chapter, linking it with previous two chapters, the destitute man buying bread, a link with Wilsons who have no money*
16 — *Tom's encounter with used car salesman (ch. 16) is a link with man buying bread (ch. 15). Casy's comments on perceived "nervousness" links with past few chapters.*
17 — *Migrant camp life described (ch. 17) links with Joads and Wilsons now traveling together*
18— *Arrival in California, Noah breaks up family (ch. 18); prophecy of man returning from California (ch. 17) begins to prove true; end of second part of novel*
19 — *Part 3 begins with ch. 19; early history of California linked to new settlers (Okies)*
20 — *Joads in first Hooverville (ch. 20); Connie abandons wife; Casy goes to jail for Tom. Abstract problems of Okies (ch. 19) become Joads' problems (ch. 20).*
21 — *Chapter 21 outlines the anger of the migrants over their treatment by the landowners. We have just seen this in the Joad family (ch. 20).*

22 — *In contrast to the dismal scenario (ch. 21), ch. 22 brings the first hope of humanity for the Joads. They arrive at the government camp and begin to feel human again.*

23 — *Ch. 23 describes the simple pleasures of the migrants relegated to the government camps such as Weedpatch (ch. 22).*

24 — *The general dancing (ch. 23) leads to the incident at the Weedpatch dance (ch. 24).*

25 — *This is another transition chapter. The Weedpatch idyl is about to end; ch. 25 contrasts the bountiful harvest and the injustice to the farm workers whose labor brought the harvest.*

26 — *The Joads leave (ch. 26) because there is no work; life gets hard again—as prophesied (ch. 25). Joads' fortunes begin to dive: Casy is killed, Tom kills Casy's assailant and goes into hiding. The family shares a boxcar with Wainwrights.*

27 — *The hard times of the cotton pickers (ch. 27) is a reflection on the previous hardships of the Joads (ch. 26).*

28 — *The end of ch. 27 (small income buying sidemeat) is a link with the relatively optimistic situation of Joads at the beginning of ch. 28. They at least have a boxcar shelter. Rainy season begins (in contrast to drought at novel's beginning). Chapter ends with Tom's leaving and utter poverty of family.*

29 — *Bleak conditions of migrants: no work, no food, steady rain; link with previous chapter's story of Joads*

30 — *The flood of ch. 30 was foreshadowed in ch. 29; Rose of Sharon's baby stillborn; Al goes with Agnes' family. The final plight of the Joads seems hopeless.*

3. **Handout 6** is a very good opportunity for students to trace an image pattern throughout an entire, complex novel. They should be instructed to write a brief note for the animal or machine references they find, along with the page where it was discovered. This exercise will be used again with **Handout 24** when the novel is completed.

Suggested Answers (among many)

		Machines	Animals
Chapter	9	selling their farm machinery at a loss	sell horse
	10	Truck becomes "living principle" of family.	Al "might be a musking goat sometimes" 2 pet dogs; leave one with Muley and take other one
	11	ode to tractors	comparison of horses and plows; Cats, mice, and weasels take over farm after Okies leave
	12	Trucks and cars fill Hwy. 66; car problems reflect migrants' precarious position on road; sedan picks up destitute family (contrast to heartlessness of others in first chapters).	

	Machines	Animals
13	Hudson begins chapter—Al has become "soul of the car."	Gila monster comparison; dog gets killed by car; dog howls at the end of chapter; field mice scamper about mattresses
14	black bombers; bank wants tractors not families on land; tractors turn multiple furrows in the vacant land.	"Western states nervous as horses before a thunderstorm" "when prisoners are struck like pigs"
15	dialogue in diner about cars: Cords, LaSalle, Cadillac, Zephyr, Buick, Ford contrast between the big car of wealthy couple and 1926 Nash; juke box, slot machine; cars whiz "viciously"	waitresses screech like a peacock; Big Bill the Rat; "you might have been a haddock;" driver in accident left "a-wigglin' like a frog on a hook;" boys leaped like chipmunks.
16	Touring car and truck travel as "unit"— problem with car takes up much of the action of chapter.	Family "like a bunch of cows when the lobos are ranging, stick all together." Tom ran down a girl "like a rabbit." Al tries to hit cat in the road but misses; jackrabbit is hit by car.
17	Cars crawled onto great highway.	Migrants scuttled like bugs, clustered bugs; rattlesnake scares horses and harrow kills farmer. Migrants crawled out like bugs.
18	Hudson Super Six sounds like a threshing machine.	Flies buzz over Granma, prayers' voices like screams of hyena, howl of a wolf, feral howling; whining like that of a litter of puppies; a food dish;
19	more tractors and machines bought by owners	noise of crickets and hum of flies; boy squirmed into the water like a muskrat; Tom kills rattler. Man must crawl like a bug between rows of lettuce. "They'd shoot us like rats;" Migrants are "rattlesnakes," like ants scurrying for work.
20	cars in camp identified by name (Model T Ford and Model A roadster), old Buick, "16" (truck); Chevrolet coupe	"My folks ain't no sheep;" People are "beating their wings like a bird in a attic; gonna bust their wings on a dusty winda tryin' to get out;"
21	industrial life "ridiculous" to migrants	On the highways the people moved like ants; hunting cats on the road;
22	flush toilets, cars and used car lots discussed	Connie can travel "jackrabbit-quick and fox sneaky." Sandry howls like an animal; Ma sees ducks and birds fly south (early winter coming).
23		"Injuns slick as snakes;" slain Indian like cock pheasant, "wasn't no bigger'n a bug;" preacher paced like a tiger.

	Machines	Animals
24	Car holds troublemakers and deputies.	dream of a little truck [farm] and a "couple pigs and some chickens;" dance to "Chicken Reel;" girls lively "as a filly in season;" Wasps, flies, and yellowjackets eat fruit too cheap to pick; pigs killed rather than given to hungry;
26	Al gets truck ready again. "You [Al] think you're just hell on wheels," flush toilets again	People build weed shacks "just like gophers;" Al kills gopher snake (harmless); Store manager has nose like a bird's beak; friendly cat identified with man who shows kindness over sugar sale; man in tent "nervous as a cat;"
27		tow cotton bags along like a work horse; "Depression is over. I seen a jackrabbit an' they wasn't nobody after him." "He don't feel no worse'n if he killed a skunk."
28	in boxcar (train stopped)	Tom "livin' like a rabbit;" Al a "dunghill rooster;" The children "came out of their beds like hermit crabs from shells."
29	coroners' wagons	Starving men steal chickens.
30	Men worked jerkily, like machines.	Children ask for pets in new house.

Assignment: Have first ten chapters read.

Finding the Links

Of the 30 chapters of *The Grapes of Wrath*, 16 are considered "intercalary"; i.e., they do not deal with the story of the Joads specifically, but they provide a broader social and historic background for the story. Beginning with chapter 1, which establishes themes and sets the mood and setting for the story, the novel's plot is interrupted by the odd-numbered chapters, except midway through the novel, when they occur at chapters 11, 12, 14, and 15. While early critics believed these chapters were mere distractions, more recent critics discovered important links between the chapters.

In preceding handouts, you explored the color and sound imagery that connected chapters 1 and 2, as well as the physical similarities between the turtle and Jim Casy. In chapter 5, Steinbeck fuses these three into the image of the "monster," his word for the Bank/Company or tractors which drive the farmers from their land.

1. List words or phrases from the novel which describe the following:

   a) Bank/Company   b) Owners

   c) Tractors   d) Man driving tractor

2. What seems to be the connecting link between the Bank, the owners, the tractors, and the driver?

3. What motivates Joe Davis's son to perform such an unpopular task?

4. In the last paragraph of chapter 5, when the tractor crumbles the tenant's house, what four words describe its final fall?

5. Where have we seen this image before?

Name _____

Date _____

What's That Again?

1. Chapter 6 opens with an obvious link to something which happens in chapter 5. Identify.

2. When Tom releases the turtle (chapter 6), in which direction does it crawl?

3. Can you think of a reason why Steinbeck gives names to the young men whose tractors destroy the tenants' homes? the used car salesmen?

4. Chapter 7 is written in what critic Peter Lisca calls "harsh, staccato prose."[1] Can you think of a reason why Steinbeck may have written this chapter on selling used cars in this hectic prose?

5. Chapter 7 tells of people buying used cars from unscrupulous salesmen. What link exists between chapter 7 and 8?

---

[1]Peter Lisca, *The Wide World of John Steinbeck* (New Brunswick, NJ: Rutgers Univ. Press, 1958), 163.

6. In the following columns make a note of the links you find between chapters and notice Steinbeck's use throughout succeeding chapters of the image patterns of people/machines/animals. Keep a record of these references on **Handout 6** for a later assignment.

Chapter	Link with Preceding Chapter
9	
10	
11	
12	
13	
14	
15	
16	
17	
18	
19	

Name _____

Date _____

Chapter	Link with Preceding Chapter
20	
21	
22	
23	
24	
25	
26	
27	
28	
29	
30	

Long-Term Project

Directions:

Since this novel is filled with references to persons, jot down the references you find in the novel to machines or animals. This handout will be used later as a way of seeing the novel as a unified whole. Begin your search with chapter 9.

Chapter	Page	Machine References	Animal References

Name _____

Date _____

Chapter	Page	Machine References	Animal References

Lesson 3
Identification of Characters and Their Philosophies

Objectives

- To explore values of the characters through their dialogue
- To have students examine their own values
- To understand the novel's characterization
- To provide an opportunity for developing writing skills

Notes to the Teacher

The exercises in this lesson will enable students to identify with the Joads and to better understand the main characters in the novel before beginning the second part.

Procedure

1. Students will have read to chapter 10 when this lesson begins. You may assign **Handout 7** to be completed out of class or do it in class. It will be a good way to discuss the values of the novel to use for class discussion.

   Suggested Answers:

   1. *Jim Casy—Casy is not a religiously orthodox man. He is outside of organized religion and its precepts.*
   2. *Davis boy—selfish, rationalizes his insensitivity to other Okies*
   3. *Muley Graves—unselfish, good person—one of "Steinbeck's speakers" in novel*
   4. *Casy—strong identification with Nature*
   5. *Grampa—hedonist, toned down as he got older; a "Bacchanalian" character*
   6. *Ma Joad—has strong opinions, much family pride, basically a generous and good character*

2. **Handout 8** may be completed in or out of class as well. You may decide to do questions 1–3 in class, use part of the class period to allow students to share their responses, and then assign the essay as an out-of-class, 4–5 paragraph composition.

3. Collect the composition from **Handout 8. Handout 9** works well as a group project. Allow students to use their texts to find phrases that describe characters. This exercise reviews the first part of the novel.

   Suggested Answers:

Grampa	"lean ragged, quick old man"; whacks himself at jokes; earthy, vulgar man; "lean, excitable face with little bright eyes as evil as a frantic child's eyes," "a cantankerous, complaining, mischievous, laughing face," lecherous, vicious, and cruel
Granma	mean as Grampa, has "a shrill ferocious religiosity, as lecherous and savage as Grampa
Uncle John	a loner, older than Pa, "crazy kind of son-of-a-bitch," "just gets stringier and meaner ever' year, meaner'n Grampa; not happy, gives things to kids to make up for guilt at wife's death
Noah	first born, tall and strange, always calm and puzzled, never angry, no sexual urges; Pa pulled his head out of shape at birth
Tom	not over 30, very dark brown eyes, high wide cheekbones, kept lips closed, dressed in new clothes that don't fit, minds his own business
Rose of Sharon	braided hair made an ash-blond crown, round, soft face, self-sufficient smile, plump (pregnant) body

Ruthie	*12, just developing breasts, "a little serious in young-ladiness"*
Winfield	*10, "a trifle of a snot nose," "kid-wild and calfish"*
Connie	*19, good hard worker, proud, frightened and bewildered at Rose of Sharon, sharp-faced, lean (Texas strain), pale blue eyes*
Jim Casy	*thin, tenor voice; long, bony head "set on a neck as stringy and muscular as a celery stalk"; beaked, hard nose; brown eyes; has "baptized look" in his eyes*

4. **Handout 10** allows creative students to blossom. By giving this exercise as an out-of-class assignment, you will provide your class a fresh way of looking at the novel. Class discussion on the day assignment is due will allow students to share in the creativity of their classmates. (It will also provide an opportunity for students to read ahead.)

Assignment: Read chapters 11–16; add to **Handouts 5** and **6**.

Name _____

Date _____

The Language of the Heart

Directions:

Identify the speakers of the lines from Column A. The chapter in which they can be found is in parentheses after the quotation. In Column B, tell what the words indicate about the speaker's philosophy or values.

Column A	Column B

1. "There ain't no sin and there ain't no virtue. There's just stuff people do. It's all part of the same thing. And some of the things folks do is nice, and some ain't nice, but that's as far as any man got a right to say." (4)

2. "Times are changed, don't you know? Thinking about stuff like that don't feed the kids. Get your three dollars a day, feed your kids. You got no call to worry about anybody's kids but your own." (5)

3. "What I mean, if a fella's got somepin to eat an' another fella's hungry-why the first fella ain't got no choice [but to share]." (6)

4. "I ain't sayin' I'm like Christ, ... But I got tired like Him, an' I got mixed up like Him, an' I went into the wilderness like Him, without no campin' stuff. . . . There was the hills, an' there was me, an' we wasn't separate no more. We was one thing. An' that one thing was holy." (8)

5. "Well, I am [a heller], kinda. But ain't nowheres near the fella I was. Jus' let me get out California, where I can pick me an orange when I want it. Or grapes. There's one thing I ain't never had enough of. Gonna get me a whole big bunch of grapes off a bush, or whatever, an' I'm gonna squash 'em on my face an' let 'em run offin my chin." (8)

Column A   Column B

6. "It ain't kin we? It's will we [take Casy along]?" she said firmly. `As far as `kin,' why, we'll do what we will . . . . I never heerd tell of no Joads or no Hazletts, neither, ever refusin' food and shelter or a lift on the road to anybody that asked. They's been mean Joads, but never that mean." (10)

Name _____

Date _____

Losses: "The Thousand Pictures"

"How can we live without our lives? How will we know it's us without our past? No. Leave it. Burn it." (ch. 9)

In chapter 9 Steinbeck pictures the migrants about to leave for California sorting through their possessions, deciding on what to take on the journey. Although each object brought with it a host of memories and an identity, the migrants had little room to carry beloved treasures.

1. Make a quick inventory of the items that identify *you*, whether they be recent acquisitions or things you have had since childhood.

2. What three things in the above list are your three favorites?

3. If you could save only one object should fire or flood strike, what would it be?

4. In a brief essay, explain your rationale for the final choices of question 2 and the one *favorite* object of question 3 and why that would be your choice.

Name _____

Date _____

A "Fambly" Photo

By chapter 10, we've met the entire Joad clan from Grandfather William James Joad to the as yet unborn child of Rose of Sharon Joad Rivers. Throughout the first part of this novel (Ch. 1–10), Steinbeck has taken great pains to describe the land of Oklahoma: once red as blood, then depleted by poor farming practices, now dry and lifeless. In the same way, the author has produced sharp verbal images of the novel's main characters, from their physical features to their mannerisms—and, in a few cases, their eccentricities. Before the Joads leave for California, take a group photograph in words, capturing as best you can each of the following characters:

Character	Physical Description
Grampa	
Granma	
Uncle John	

Name _____

Date _____

Character	Physical Description
Noah	
Tom	
Rose of Sharon	
Ruthie	
Winfield	

Name _____

Date _____

Character	Physical Description
Connie	
Jim Casy	

Name _____

Date _____

A Going Away Gift

Having reviewed the novel's characters and studied their actions, try your hand at a creative departure gift for the Joads.

Since Steinbeck uses color imagery so effectively in the novel, try to choose a *color* that expresses to you the essence of each of the characters, and in Column B give a brief rationale for your choice.

A second possibility is to choose a *sound* (e.g., of a musical instrument) that represents a particular character for you, the composite of which would create a symphonic gift for the Joads. A third possibility might be particular *flowers* that symbolize for you each of the novel's characters to form a bouquet.

Directions:

Choose any *one* of the above categories and follow through with a color, sound, or flower for each of the characters, followed by a few words to explain your choice.

A	B
Grampa	
Granma	
Uncle John	

Name _____

Date _____

A	B
Pa	
Ma	
Noah	
Tom	
Al	

A	B
Rose of Sharon	
Ruthie	
Winfield	
Connie	
Jim Casy	

Lesson 4

A Time to Change: Motifs in the Novel

Objectives

- To explore the question of what it means to be human in a world of machines
- To identify and discuss several types of prejudice in the novel
- To encourage students to reflect upon stereotypes and labels
- To help students to see the relevance of Steinbeck's story today

Notes to the Teacher

This unit provides a good opportunity for students to explore the role of technology in their lives. For the average high school student, technology is a "given"—but they seldom question the ramifications of technology in the world of manufacturing, medicine, or information accessibility. Steinbeck wrote this novel before the computer revolution, but he was never an anti-machine agrarian purist. He saw machines, rightly, as offering possibilities for a better life for all people. Students will have an opportunity with this unit to explore a major theme of the novel: the consequences of excluding the poor from the power that machine ownership brings.

Handout 13 is one of the most important of this unit for "bringing the novel home." Steinbeck's portrayal of the poor in this book wins our sympathy, and it is important to have students see that the Joads we now know (and identify with) are seen as dirty and uncivilized by the people still rooted to their lands or towns. Helping students to connect the Okies with the poor they may encounter is the goal of this unit.

Procedure

1. Have students take out **Handout 10** and use it as a basis for class discussion.

2. Distribute **Handout 11** and allow students (preferably in small groups) to answer the question posed about the "machine man."

Suggested Answers

a) *He has no "wonder" in his work, loses understanding of relationship between people and land, is contemptuous of the land and of himself.*

b) *Answers will vary.*

3. **Handout 12** may be given as an out-of-class assignment or an in-class group assignment.

Suggested Answers

1. *They have had to leave their farm and Oklahoma; they have added Casy and Wilsons to "extended family"; Grampa dies; their pet dog is hit by a car.*

2. *Ma seems to be opening her concept of family (allowing Casy and Wilsons in); Tom seems to be reflecting on Casy's message of universal compassion for fellow human beings.*

3. *Our only way to survive as a human race is to shift from total independence to inter-dependence.*

4. *Yes. Answers will vary for second part. We don't know, can only hope she will. As number of migrants gets larger, the residents tend to get more hard-hearted, not less—as a means of survival.*

4. **Handout 13** may be assigned ahead of class period and used as a basis for class discussion.

Suggested Answers

1. *Answers will vary.*

2. *Yes, usually.*

3. *They hate the influx of migrants to their states, and we tend to use derogatory names for those we dislike, fear, or look down upon.*

4. *Because "red" meant "troublemaker," owners or bosses would call people who asked a fair wage by that name.*

5. *No. Yes.*

6. *Answers will vary.*
7. *They all put down the person who is called the name.*
8. *Yes. It is hoped that students have a different "mind's eye view" of the Joads.*

9. *Answers will vary.*
10. *Answers will vary.*

Assignment: Read Chs. 17–22; add to **Handouts 5** and **6.**

The Machine Age Comes to Oklahoma

"The family met at the most important place, near the truck. The house was dead, and the fields were dead; but this truck was the active thing, the living principle. The ancient Hudson, with bent and scarred radiator screen, with grease in dusty globules at the worn edge of every moving part, with hub caps gone and caps of red dust in their places-this was the new hearth, the living center of the family; half passenger car and half truck, high-sided and clumsy." (ch. 10)

The novel begins with a poetic tribute to the land and its people. In chapter 2 the red, living earth is replaced by a roaring, huge red truck. Every chapter but 4 contains references to cars, trucks, or tractors. Yet, as in the passage above, not all the references are negative. Machines have come to replace the land and the farm as America becomes a nation on the move.

Steinbeck's ambivalence towards machines (and America's future in 1939) is captured by the passage in chapter 11, paragraph one, in which he ponders the age-old question: What does it mean to be human in a world that is becoming increasingly mechanized?

Read the opening paragraphs of chapter 11 and summarize the major points the narrator makes about the new "machine man."

Do you agree with this analysis more than fifty years later?

From "I" to "We"

"Times are changing, mister, don't you know?" (ch. 5)

"Seems to me we don't never come to nothin'. Always on the way." (ch. 13)

"Thus they changed their social life—changed as in the whole universe only man can change."

"The Western land, nervous under the beginning change. The Western States nervous as horses before a thunder storm. The great owners, nervous, sensing a change, knowing nothing of the nature of the change." (ch. 14)

"They's gonna come a thing that's gonna change the whole country." (ch. 16)

"For here 'I lost my land' is changed; a cell is split and from its splitting grows the thing you hate—'We lost *our* land.' . . . This is the beginning—from 'I' to 'we.'" (ch. 14)

From the first pages of this novel, the reader senses a change has come over the land. The red earth is turned to gray dust. The tenant farmers are pushed off their land and onto Highway 66 by debts and greedy owners. We see characters change, such as the service station owner of chapter 13, who begins as a whining worrier and ends up showing compassion when the Joads' dog is run over, offering to "bury 'im out in the corn field."

But one of the biggest changes is in the "fambly" unit itself. For Ma, this is the one constant in a world of change. Yet the changes in the family have already begun—and will continue.

1. List first a few changes you have seen in the Joads' circumstances, family structure, etc. from the time the novel opens.

2. List any changes you have noted in the *attitudes* of any of the Joad family.

3. The final quotation above captures the major theme of Steinbeck's novel (the movement from "I" to "we"). Can you summarize briefly what you think this quotation means?

4. Does Mae have a change of heart in chapter 15? Will she treat future poor people who enter the restaurant any differently? Why or why not?

"Sticks 'n Stones": Looking at Ourselves and Others

"Well, Okie use' to mean you was from Oklahoma. Now it means you're a dirty son-of-a-bitch. Okie means you're scum. Don't mean nothing itself, it's the way they say it." (ch. 18)

"A red is any son-of-a-bitch that wants thirty cents an hour when we're payin' twenty-five." (ch. 22)

"Them Okies? They're all hard-lookin."

"Well, you and me got sense. Them goddamn Okies got no sense and no feeling. They ain't human. A human being wouldn't live like they do. A human being couldn't stand it to be so dirty and miserable. They ain't a hell of a lot better than gorillas." (ch. 18)

"Sure they talk the same language, but they ain't the same. Look how they live. Think any of us folks'd live like that? Hell no!" (ch. 19)

"These goddamned Okies are dirty and ignorant. They're degenerate, sexual maniacs. Those goddamned Okies are thieves. They'll steal anything. They've got no sense of property rights."

And the latter was true, for how can a man without property know the ache of ownership? And the defending people said, "They bring disease, they're filthy. We can't have them in the schools. They're strangers. How'd you like to have your sister go out with one of 'em?" (ch. 21)

1. Most of us grew up chanting the nursery rhyme that ends, "Words will never hurt you," but our experience has proved that words can hurt every bit as much as sticks and stones. Can you remember a time when someone called you a name and it truly hurt?

2. Does it hurt more when the name-calling is done by persons we know (or love) rather than strangers?

3. In the first quotation above, a returning migrant explains to Tom that Okie was not always a term of derision but now its meaning has changed. What changed the meaning of the word?

4. At various points in the novel, people deemed "troublemakers" are called "reds," "bolsheviks," or communists. In the second quotation, an owner named Hines attempts to define "reds" for the curious young man. Explain what his definition means.

5. Do Americans today have a common definition for "communist"? Do we ever use the word in the same way Steinbeck's characters used "Okies"?

6. Can you think of other labels that are in everyday use?

7. What do the labels have in common?

8. In the last two quotations, we overhear people discussing the poor, hungry migrants before them. Might these people have been the Joads? Is this how you have seen them in your mind's eye as you read the novel?

9. In your experience, do people often believe that poor people, who do not look (or smell) as good as they themselves do, *are* somehow subhuman, unfeeling, stupid creatures.

10. Has reading *The Grapes of Wrath* changed any of your perceptions about the poor and homeless of *our* time? Explain.

Lesson 5

History of America According to John Steinbeck

Objectives

- To sharpen students' sense of history
- To enable students to correlate the Dust Bowl with present ecological concerns
- To develop students' understanding of the American Dream
- To help students recognize the theme of the American Dream in *The Grapes of Wrath*
- To practice writing skills

Notes to the Teacher

Steinbeck, as the quotation at the beginning of **Handout 14** illustrates, was "trying to write history while it was happening," and he didn't "want to be wrong." Chapter 19 of the novel attempts to link California's past with the present as he was experiencing it. As high school students often exhibit limited skills in history, this novel affords the opportunity to make history come alive for them and to illustrate the connections between the past and the present.

This lesson also enables students to study the literary concept of the American Dream. For some, it will be yet another example, but for others this may be the first time they have encountered the term. Teachers should adjust the presentation of the lesson to the particular class's background.

Procedure

1. Since students have already read chapter 19, before distributing **Handout 14**, briefly review the barbarian invasions of Europe as a way of understanding Steinbeck's analogy in question 4. It might also be advantageous to use this point to discuss the advantages of a strong historical background to help students comprehend novels and world events. The educated reader usually appreciates—and enjoys—more what he or she reads.

2. **Handout 14** may be done individually or as a group assignment. In either procedure, it will provide fruitful discussion.

Suggested Answers

1. *Answers will vary.*
2. *They see that some people owned more land than they need; they have none.*
3. *This should provide a spirited discussion. Answers will hinge on how students answered question 2.*
4. *The barbarians disrupted the civilizations they invaded. The Okies threaten the landowners because they are desperate.*
5. *land and food*
6. *Any time people are hungry, landless, and at the bottom of the social ladder, they have the potential to rise up and take what has not been shared with them. Steinbeck was a "prophet" who saw the future uprisings in the South as ultimately inevitable.*
7. *When the people stop relying on God to change the hearts of the rich and take matters into their own hands, the "end" of the status quo will arrive, bringing violence and social upheaval in its wake.*

3. **Handout 15** should not be an excuse to see the Joads as totally responsible for their own catastrophe, but it is a chance to discuss our sometimes thoughtless or selfish use of the earth's resources, with little vision of the long-term consequences of our actions. Discuss current ecological concerns and students' attitudes toward the environment before distributing **Handout 15**. Questions can be answered as total class project.

Suggested Answers

1. "It robs it, sucks all the blood out of it."
2. It was a fast cash crop; they were tenants and the owners wanted profit.
3. Poor see war (and violent death of others) as a way out of death by starvation. They fail to see an alternative between two modes of violence.
4. a) Yes, people who owned munitions factories, aircraft companies, those who worked overtime in the steel mills;
   b) the ones who were killed, injured, or left homeless by war

4. Review concept of American Dream by recalling other stories students may have studied (e.g., *The Great Gatsby*). Emphasize that, as in all dreams, sometimes the thing we think will bring us the most pleasure turns out to be a nightmare. The romantic quest for a piece of land to call one's own lies at the heart of the early American frontier experience. (Today, for example, we refer to the "new frontier," outer space). In *Of Mice and Men* and *Grapes of Wrath* in particular, Steinbeck's portrayal is that of the American Dream gone awry. This portion of Lesson 5 enables students to examine America's dream of unlimited resources and the reality of a fragile earth, polluted and abused by exploitation and thoughtlessness.

5. Distribute **Handout 16** and assign essay to be completed out of class.

Assignment: Complete reading of novel. Write essay. Add to **Handouts 5** and **6**.

Enrichment Exercise: If students have already studied Fitzgerald's novel, they may be assigned an essay comparing the treatment of the American Dream in *Gatsby* and *Grapes of Wrath*, or in *The Adventures of Huckleberry Finn*.

Links with the Past and the Future

"I suppose I could dash [*The Grapes of Wrath*] off, but I want this one to be a pretty good one. There's another difficulty, too. I'm trying to write history while it is happening and I don't want to be wrong." *(Letters,* p. 162)

Steinbeck's chapter 19 tells the story of California from the days when it belonged to Mexico, through the "invasion" of the early settlers in the Gold Rush days, through the era of cheap, foreign workers, to the 20th century when the Joads arrive.

1. Steinbeck compares this early Western history to that of Rome and the barbarian invasions. Do you agree with Steinbeck's analogy?

2. Why do the dispossessed migrants believe that they had as much right to the land as the earlier settlers?

3. Do you agree? Why or why not?

4. Steinbeck describes the migrants as dangerous "new barbarians." Explain.

5. What two things do the "Okies" want?

6. The author describes these people "as dangerous as niggers in the South!" What relationship does the Depression migration to California have to the civil rights era of the Sixties in the South? (Remember that the novel was written in 1939. Was Steinbeck a prophet or did he see the same seeds of explosive change in the South of the late Thirties as he saw in the West?)

7. Chapter 19 ends with a prayer by the narrator of the novel and an ominous final two sentences:

> And the association of owners knew that some day
> the praying would stop.
> And there's the end.

Explain what you think these final lines mean.

The Dust Bowl of the Thirties

We tend to think that America was always the way it is now—and that it will always be this way. But a study of history shows that early American maps included in the "Great American Desert" much of the Western Range, including the plains in the western parts of Nebraska, Kansas, and Texas.[1] With increased rainfall, settlers believed that the land could be cultivated, but serious widespread drought in the middle of the 1880s culminated in the great drought of 1894 and 1895. The "wet years" from 1905 to 1915 brought false confidence.[2] By the 1930s, farmers were once again caught up in the Dust Bowl, which provides the catalyst for the Joads' journey westward to California, "the land flowing with milk and honey," the Promised Land.

No one can read Steinbeck's novel without feeling sympathy for the farmers who lost their farms to the great drought, but a close reading of the novel reveals that the Joads and their neighbors sometimes were not good stewards of their farmland.

In chapter 4, for example, Tom tells Casy, "Ever' year I can remember, we had a good crop comin' an' it never come. Grampa says she was good the first five plowin's, while the wild grass was still in her." Two chapters later, Muley tells Tom, "I know this land ain't much good. Never was much good 'cept for grazin'. Never should a broke her up. And now she's cottoned near to death." And in the intercalary chapter 5, we find this dialogue between a land owner and a sharecropper;

"But you'll kill the land with cotton."
"We know. We've got to take cotton quick before the land dies. Then we'll sell the land.
Lots of families in the East would like to own a piece of land."

1. How does Steinbeck describe what cotton does to the soil? (ch. 5, par. 5)

2. Why did the farmers turn from growing grain to cotton?

[1]Ivan Ray Tannehill, "Dusters and Black Blizzards," in *A Companion to The Grapes of Wrath*, Ed. Warren French (New York: Viking Press, 1963).
[2]*Ibid.*, 6–7

3. What is the irony of the following passage, written in 1939?

> "The squatting men raised their eyes to understand. Can't we just hang on? Maybe the next year will be a good year. God knows how much cotton next year. And with all the wars—God knows what price cotton will bring. Don't they make explosives out of cotton? And uniforms? Get enough wars and cotton'll hit the ceiling. Next year, maybe." (ch. 5)

4. Do people sometimes prosper in wartime? Who prospered in World War II? Who didn't?

Name _____

Date _____

The American Dream Reconsidered

"Wait till we get to California. You'll see nice country then."

"Jesus Christ, Pa! This here is California." (ch. 18)

From earliest times American settlers were lured westward. The promise of land owner-ship and independence inspired Eastern families to pack all their belongings into a covered wagon and head out to the Midwest and eventually California. Most of the early settlers were small farmers. They cleared the land, built cabins, raised their families in near isola-tion. The American Dream of land and freedom, however, was elusive from the start.

Many settlers died on the journey, particularly women and small children. Loneliness gnawed at the heart; hunger and disease stalked their cabins. But Americans never gave up the dream that if only they could go a little further west, life would be better. Thus, it is no surprise that the Joads and their neighbors pack up their belongings and head for Cali-fornia, where the handbills promise jobs, plenty of fruit, and a chance to escape foreclosure and dispossession.

When the Joads reach California, however, the promise of a new life is short-lived. Cali-fornia is lush and beautiful, but it is never theirs. Just as the banks took over the farms back home, the California farms are owned by corporations, which, like the banks, have no faces.

And now there is no more "West" to go to. California is the last frontier, the end of the journey, the last hope for the Joads and the other migrants—or is it?

Louis Owens, in *John Steinbeck's Re-Vision of America,* offers another possibility: *"The Grapes of Wrath* both condemns the illusion of Eden and offers a way out of the wasteland created by that illusion."[1] The *new* dream is commitment—to the land and to one another. The Joads learn that the "fambly" isn't enough. The land of Oklahoma has been destroyed and now the dispossessed migrants must travel to a new land *and* a new understanding of the relationship between land and humankind. It is a lesson we still must learn.

Time magazine (Jan. 2, 1989), bypassing its usual Man/Woman of the Year award, chose instead as 1988's most newsworthy "person" the Endangered Earth, Planet of the Year. *Time* justified the unorthodox choice by explaining that "environmental disasters-droughts, floods, forest fires, polluted beaches-dominated the [year's] news" (p. 3).

What is the connection between Steinbeck's story of the drought of the 1930s (depleted soil, poor farming methods, displacement of peoples) and the plight of American farmers or Third-World residents today?

Having done some research on the topic, write a brief essay, describing not only the con-nections you see, but (if possible) what solutions you would offer that ought to be considered by world and national leaders.

[1]Louis Owens, *John Steinbeck's Re-Vision of America* (Athens, Ga.: Univ. of Georgia Press, 1985), 129.

Lesson 6

Steinbeck's Characters: A Sharp Ear and a Good Eye for People

Objectives

- To make inferences from textual clues
- To explore the roles of women and men in this novel

Notes to the Teacher

This lesson reinforces students' understanding of the major (and some minor) characters in this novel.

Procedure

1. Elicit responses to the question: "Would you have liked to be one of the women in *The Grapes of Wrath*?" Why or why not? Discussion should be lively and indicate how well students have understood the novel, revealing many of their attitudes concerning sexual roles in society.

2. Distribute **Handout 17.** Discuss individual quotations from the novel and have students complete the exercise.

    Suggested Answers

    1. *Ma keeps family together, is heart and soul of the family (the "citadel"), supplants Pa as head of the family as it begins to disintegrate.*
    2. *Rose of Sharon probably doesn't exhibit any leadership or strength until the novel's end when she feeds the dying man with her breast.*
    3. *Students may disagree about Mae. She is vain, a flirt, and a snob. Yet she does show compassion to the children of the poor man trying to buy a loaf of bread.*
    4. *Mrs. Wilson, although dying of cancer, is compassionate at Grampa's death, offering shelter and a blanket to bury him.*
    5. *Mrs. Wainwright, like Ma Joad, seems to be the center of her family. She assists at the birth of Rose of Sharon's stillborn.*

    6. *Lisbeth Sandry may not get many votes for compassion or sensitivity, but some may see her at least as a "moral" character. Steinbeck, however, seems to provide her as a type of the aggressive, self-righteous bigot that did not possess "true religion."*

3. Point out that **Handout 18** will enable students to review all the major characters as a way of remembering the plot.

4. Distribute **Handout 18.** Students may answer questions individually or within a group. This handout may be used as an evaluation tool to determine how well students comprehend the novel. Completed handouts may be collected instead of being immediately used as a vehicle for discussion.

    Suggested Answers

    1. *Uncle John is, in some ways, a link with the outsiders to the Joads' immediate family. At another level, his preoccupation with sin and guilt provides a philosophical contrast to Casy's relativism about sin.*
    2. *Grampa represents the earthy life-force of the Joads. He's so much a part of the land that he dies when he's uprooted.*
    3. *Answers will vary. Although stubborn, Pa seems to become weaker as each chapter progresses. Not until he rallies the men to build the dike in the final chapter does he seem to shake off his lethargy.*
    4. a) *Tom carries Casy's (Steinbeck's ?) philosophy into the world of the migrants after Casy's death. He provides hope that the movement*

from "I" to "we" may become a reality.

   b) You could because he changes more than any other character in the novel.

5. *Even critics disagree on this one. Casy is "real" at many levels, but sometimes he seems to be more a walking philosophy textbook than a flesh-and-blood character. On the other hand, he is central to the theme of the novel, provides links with many of the novel's characters and events, and dies for what he believes.*

6. *Al understands machines (cars and trucks). When the war comes, it is men like Al who will benefit from their mechanical ability. The West Coast is still the center of the nation's largest air and spacecraft industry. After 1940, with more automobiles on the highway, the need for mechanics grew. Of all the characters, he is the most employable.*

Assignment: Add to **Handouts 5** and **6**.

Enrichment Exercise: You may want to compare Ma's "revolt" with Mary E. Wilkins Freeman's "The Revolt of Mother."

"A Woman's Place": A Closer Look at Steinbeck's Women Characters

Women and children knew deep in themselves that no misfortune was too great to bear if their men were whole. (ch. 1)

He [Uncle John] would have liked Rose of Sharon to sit there [next to driver]. This was impossible because she was young and a woman. (ch. 10)

The preacher stepped beside her. "Leave me salt down this meat," he said. "I can do it. There's other stuff for you to do."

She stopped her work then and inspected him oddly, as though he suggested a curious thing. And her hands were crusted with salt, pink with fluid from the fresh pork. "It's women's work," she said finally.

"It's all work.," the preacher replied. "They's too much of it to split it up to men's or women's work. You got stuff to do. Leave me salt the meat." (ch. 10)

Pa sniffed "Seems like times is changed," he said sarcastically. "Time was when a man said what we'd do. Seems like women is tellin' now. Seems like it's purty near time to get out a stick." (ch. 26)

"Women can change better'n a man . . . . Woman got all her life in her arms. Man got it all in his head." (ch. 28)

"Man, lives in jerks—baby born an' a man dies, an' that's a jerk—gets a farm, an' loses his farm, an' that's a jerk. Woman, it's all one flow, like a stream, little eddies, little waterfalls, but the river, it goes right on." (ch. 28)

While the women in this novel by custom of the time are considered socially inferior to the men, they are remarkably well drawn, with Ma Joad being perhaps the most memorable of all Steinbeck's characters. Steinbeck's main women characters are dependent but a source of strength and endurance for their men. In the space provided, list the ways you see the following characters (if you do) as exhibiting strength, leadership, or a moral center for other characters in the novel.

Ma Joad

Rose of Sharon

Mae

Mrs. Wilson

Mrs. Wainwright

Lisbeth Sandry

Name _____

Date _____

Steinbeck's Male Characters: Saints, Sinners, and In-Betweens

If Ma Joad is perhaps the character one most remembers from this novel, the male characters are no less essential to its plot. Tom and Jim Casy are prominent in the novel's opening chapters, playing the roles of prophet and tribal leader before the story ends. While the brain-damaged Noah is the first to break up the family (after the grandparents' deaths), Connie Rivers soon abandons his pregnant wife and their dreams of night school and a little house of their own.

1. What role does Uncle John play in this story? Can you justify his inclusion in the journey to California?

2. What role does Grampa play in this novel? Is it fitting that he never makes it to California? Explain.

3. In your opinion, is Pa Joad a weak or a strong character in this novel? Explain.

4. Tom, having killed a man, is paroled from prison in the novel's first chapters. He is crucial to the story line. How?

Could you justify calling him the main character of the novel? Explain.

5. Jim Casy, although not one of the Joads, joins the family in its travels westward. What role does Casy play in the story? Is he a realistic character? Why or why not?

6. Many critics see Al, Tom's "randy" younger brother, as a minor, significant character in this novel. Yet of all the characters in the story, Al has the best chance of success in California—or anywhere else in America of the '40s (and beyond). Explain why he, even more than Ruthie and Winfield, represents "the future."

Lesson 7

Religious Connections: Biblical and Mythic Roots of *The Grapes of Wrath*

Objectives

- To help students to understand the biblical references in the novel
- To examine the novel's title and discuss implications
- To explore the novel's mythic roots

Notes to the Teacher

While this may be one of the most difficult lessons in this unit, it should prove to be one of the most rewarding. Critics have argued about the significance of the biblical allusions and structure of Steinbeck's novel since its publication. For purposes of classroom use, this lesson avoids some of the more controversial questions (e.g., Casy and Tom as Christ figures, Steinbeck's attack on organized religion, etc.), but no understanding of the novel can avoid the inter-weaving of biblical themes, allusions in the title, names of characters, etc. Steinbeck's own religious orientation is not germane to the argument.

Since some comprehension of the Bible as literary reference is crucial to interpretation of works of literature, past and present, **Handout 19** will enable students to have some framework for interpreting other works they will read.

Procedure

1. Steinbeck wanted the music and all the verses of the "Battle Hymn of the Republic" printed in the first edition. One way to introduce this lesson is to play a recording of the piece and distribute the lyrics, which are easily available on the Internet. Discuss the song as an *American* hymn. Explain why it was a favorite of civil rights marchers from the Sixties to the present.

2. You may then discuss how grapes have a dual symbolism in the Bible. Sometimes they are symbols of plenty (e.g. Numbers 13:23), and sometimes they

represent suffering because they are crushed in the winepress. This winepress image is central to the paradoxical Christian message: out of death, life; out of suffering, joy. Crushed grapes become wine, biblical symbol of joy and salvation. The Israelites, living in a land where water was scarce, treasured wine with their meals, shared it with guests and travelers, and always included it in their celebrations.

3. Distribute **Handout 19** and use the first portion for continued discussion of the theme. The remainder of the questions should be completed in small groups prior to whole class discussion.

Suggested Answers:

1. *Instead of peace and prosperity, the Joads are met with hunger and violence in California. They never get the "promised land."*
2. *Rose of Sharon truly gives of herself to bring life to the dying man, who would die without the nourishment. Christ says, "I am the Bread of Life" (John 6:35).*
3. *Moses was the baby in the basket, and the irony is that he saved his people but the infant cannot tell them because he's dead. Only the sensitive hearts will see the connection between the actions that have caused the infant's death and their own selfishness.*
4. *Migrants must observe "the right of privacy in the tent; the right to keep the past black hidden in the heart; the right to talk and to listen; the right to refuse help or to accept, to offer help or to decline it; the right of a son to court and daughter to be courted; the right of the hungry to be fed; the rights of the pregnant and the sick to transcend all other rights." The "rights" to be destroyed*

were "the right to intrude upon privacy, the right to be noisy while the camp slept, the right of seduction or rape, the right of adultery and theft and murder." It was also unlawful to 'foul the drinking water or eat good rich food near one who is hungry unless he is asked to share." The Ten Commandments prohibit theft, adultery and murder, but the New Testament law of love covers many of the other "rights."

5. The correlation is, on the surface, obvious, but students may not be aware that God's "Chosen People" also often suffered greatly. That correlation should be shown as well.

6. The devil took the form of a serpent in the Garden of Eden account of Genesis. The snake here is an omen that California will not be a Paradise for them.

4. Prepare for **Handout 20** by reviewing the "truth" of myths: they are not merely made up stories about people who never lived but stories often rooted in folklore containing deep truths about humankind that remain true for each succeeding age. Students may have already studied some myths. If so, review what they already have learned. If the subject is completely new, you may want to introduce this handout by retelling one of the more popular myths, e.g., Pandora, Jason and the Golden Fleece, Prometheus, Narcissus, etc. When you are certain students understand the concept, distribute **Handout 20**. Allow students to complete this handout on their own since the assignment will involve a review of many events in the novel and will require some time.

Suggested Answers

1. Students may disagree here. One could justifiably argue that taking up the cause of the strikers and risking one's life for others requires "super-human courage."

2. Joads survive trial by fire (blistering sun, threat of being burnt out of camps), drought, and flood. They must undergo death of loved ones and a stillborn child. They suffer hunger and cold, discomfort, and a nearly hopeless life through most of the novel.

3. Again, students may disagree. Certainly Casy's philosophy gives the Joads a rationale for their suffering. Whether or not one agrees with his beliefs that "all is holy" and that we must care for one another or die, the answers here will cause students to examine their own beliefs.

4. Geographically, the Joads travel about 1,800 miles, not the world or a universe, but a vast distance nonetheless.

5. Tom hears rumors of disillusionment in ch. 10; the ragged man whose children starved meets them on his way back in ch. 16.

6. Casy and Tom get little out of their efforts for others—except death and the threat of death. Perhaps "super-human" is arguable, but Tom's remembering Casy and his words in ch. 28 are remarkably similar to the experience of the Apostles after Calvary and Easter. The Gospel was written years later, as they remembered Christ's message. The Spirit of God fills their hearts and inspires them to carry on the message (in all but one case to ultimate martyrdom). Tom's "transformation" is best seen in his dialogue with Ma in the cave in ch. 28, beginning "Well, maybe like Casy says, a fella ain't got a soul of his own, but on'y a piece of a big one—an' then—. . . ." The end of this passage reveals Casy's "transformation": "Seems like I can see him sometimes."

Assignment: Complete **Handout 20**. Add to **Handout 5** and **6**.

Steinbeck's Use of Biblical Imagery

Although Steinbeck drew the title for his novel from "The Battle Hymn of the Republic" ("He is trampling out the vintage where the grapes of wrath are stored"), Julia Ward Howe took the image from the Book of Revelation: "And the angel thrust in his sickle into the earth, and gathered the vine of the earth, and cast it into the great winepress of the wrath of God" (14:19). Study the following scriptural passages and determine if you can see any connection to the many references to grapes in the novel; e.g., Grampa's desire to squash a big bunch of grapes and let them run off his chin or chapter 25's concluding sentence: "In the souls of the people the grapes of wrath are filling and growing heavy, growing heavy for the vintage."

Deuteronomy 32:32—"Their grapes are grapes of gall, their clusters are bitter. Their wine is the poison of serpents. . . . "

Jeremiah 31:29—"The fathers have eaten sour grapes and their children's teeth are set on edge."

1. As Peter Lisca points out, the novel's three sections (drought, journey, and California) correspond to the Israelites' "oppression in Egypt, the exodus, and the sojourn in the land of Canaan, which in both accounts is first viewed from the mountains."[1] In what ways is California *not* the Promised Land for the Joads?

2. Just as the novel's title comes from the Bible, so too does Rose of Sharon's name: "I [Christ] am the rose of Sharon and the lily of the valley" (Cant. 2:1). Traditionally, this reference to Christ as Rose of Sharon is linked with another passage in the Canticles: "This thy stature is like to a palm tree and thy breasts to clusters of grapes" (7:7). In the Eucharist, Christians believe that Christ gives himself, body and blood, in the form of bread and wine. What do you see as the life-giving link in this symbolic action and the last scene of the novel?

[1]Peter Lisca, *The Wide World of John Steinbeck* (New Brunswick, N.J.: Rutgers University Press, 1958), 169.

3. When Uncle John puts Rose of Sharon's stillborn child in an old apple crate and floats it downstream, he says, "Go down and tell 'em." These words remind us of a well-known spiritual—and the ironic reference to the biblical leader who is *saved* in a basket placed in the bullrushes of Egypt. Who is the Jewish leader, and how is Steinbeck being ironic?

4. God gave the Israelites the commandments during their desert exodus. In chapter 17, the migrants develop "new laws" which the Joads are given at the government camp. What are some of the "rights" which become laws? Are they at all reminiscent of the law of Mt. Sinai? How are they alike/different?

5. Ma constantly reminds her family: "Us people will go on livin' when all them people is gone. Why, Tom, we're the people that live. They ain't gonna wipe us out. Why, we're the people—we go on" (ch. 20). Is there a correlation between her concept of "people" and the biblical People of God? Are the Joads "Chosen People"?

6. One of Steinbeck's major themes (cf. *Of Mice and Men*) is humankind's search for the Promise Land, a Garden of Eden, "flowing with milk and honey." Why is it so significant that Tom comes upon a snake in the road (and kills it) just as the Joads first see California, "the valley golden and green before them" (ch. 18)?

Name _____

Date _____

Mythic Journey Westward

Most myths are concerned with bigger-than-life heroes, who perform deeds of great valor requiring superhuman courage. The episodes of the myth are important to the history of a nation or a race. Their settings are vast, covering great nations, the world, or the universe. Myths sometimes contain prophecies of coming doom. Finally, the hero is often granted immortality as a reward for fighting injustice.

If Tom Joad is the hero of Steinbeck's novel, he hardly seems godlike in chapter 1. Yet by the end of the novel, he does achieve a mythical quality after Casy's death. Let's explore other mythical qualities of Steinbeck's novel.

1. Does Tom or Casy perform "deeds of great valor requiring superhuman courage"?

2. List the great tribulations and obstacles the Joads pass through in their journey.

3. Do Tom/Casy's actions have importance for the people of this story? or for generations yet unborn?

4. Does the setting of the novel cover a vast geographic distance?

5. Are there prophecies of impending doom in the novel? Who brings them?

6. Do Tom and Casy unselfishly fight injustice? Are Tom and Casy transformed into almost superhuman characters by the novel's end? Give evidence from the text.

Lesson 8

A Philosophical Adventure: Steinbeck's Isms

Objectives

- To broaden students' understanding of the philosophy which lies at the heart of this novel
- To explore students' personal philosophies
- To encourage critical thinking skills

Notes to the Teacher

While this lesson deals with abstractions, students should learn to read novels at many levels. The average reader looks for plot and characters when approaching a novel. The critical reader is enriched through comprehending the various philosophical stances discussed in this lesson. Moving from *who* and *what* to *why* is the hallmark of a critical thinker.

Procedure

1. If students have studied nineteenth-century American literature, they may already be acquainted with some of the classic American philosophers discussed in this lesson. Review the philosophy of Ralph Waldo Emerson, William James, and Henry David Thoreau, for example, and be sure students can define the term. (A simple definition appears in the first paragraph of **Handout 21;** you may want students to come to class with a formal definition of the term.)

2. Have students explore various philosophies which "offer insight into motives and point to the springs of action" (e.g., selfishness, altruism, honesty, pursuit of wealth over everything, etc.) Place terms on the board. Discuss how operating within each of these (and others they may add) will produce different actions in similar situations.

3. Distribute **Handout 21** and prepare students for assignment. Recommend a good dictionary or encyclopedia of philosophy to produce simple or complex definitions of the two terms in No. 1.

4. You may want to begin question 2 by having class supply representative actions of *one* of the characters listed.

5. Assign the rest of **Handout 21.**

Suggested Answers

1. a) *A reliance on the intuition and the conscience, a form of idealism; a philosophical ROMANTICISM reaching America a generation or two after it developed in Europe."*[1]

   b) *A term, first used by C. S. Peirce in 1879, describing a philosophical doctrine that determines value and meaning through the test of consequences or utility."*[2]

2. a) *Casy saves Tom from prison and offers his life for better conditions for the workers.*

   b) *Tom avenges Casy's death and chooses to follow in his footsteps, risking his life for others.*

   c) *Ma is a true nurturer, always looking out for her family and eventually for members of the human family.*

   d) *Rose of Sharon offers her breast to a dying stranger.*

   e) *The Wilsons offer their tent and blanket for a decent death and burial for Grampa.*

   f) *The Wainrights form a bond with the Joads through Agnes and Al's relationship. They share what they have, helping Rose of Sharon in childbirth.*

3. *Tom is part of the Oversoul, bound to those especially who are the least in the society. He is committed to seeking justice for the oppressed.*

---

[1]C. Hugh Holman and William Horman. *A Handbook to Literature,* 5th ed. (New York: Macmillan. 1986), 509.
[2]Ibid., 391.

6. Have students take out **Handout 21** for class discussion.

7. Students may already be familiar with the terms Naturalism and Realism, but a review would help even those who can identify the terms. There are many ways to introduce this handout. You might give students an overview of the influence of Charles Darwin on British and American literature or choose a work they have already studied as a springboard to *The Grapes of Wrath*, e.g., *The Red Badge of Courage* or *Call of the Wild*.

8. Distribute **Handout 22**. After you are sure students understand the concept of Naturalism, allow students to work in groups to complete the handout.

9. Use the handout to compare groups' responses and lead students to see that "labeling" a novel is as risky and wrong-headed as labeling a person. Few novels are so clearly classified.

Suggested Answers

Examples of Naturalism

1. *natural disasters in novel over which toads have little control (e.g., flood, drought);*
2. *the Joad family itself, which leads a "natural" life, especially the Grandparent Joads;*
3. *Casy's "sermons" on oneness with nature, holiness in life itself ('All that lives is holy.");*
4. *emphasis of the natural over the supernatural throughout novel*
5. *numerous correlations between animals and people in the novel*

Choices, decisions

1. *Casy's decision to give himself up to save Tom from prison*
2. *Tom breaks parole to travel with family, chooses to take up Casy's work after his death.*
3. *The Wallaces of Weedpatch share their work with Tom.*
4. *Mae's giving candy below cost to father of hungry children*
5. *Rose of Sharon's unselfishness at the novel's end*

10. Ask volunteers to share additional decisions.

11. Like the previous two handouts of this lesson **Handout 23** needs some preparation time. The word *Marxist* for some students will immediately bring to mind *Communist*; for others, the word will have no recognition at all. Early critics were more likely to categorize Steinbeck and his novel as Marxist. Today's critics almost unanimously read the novel as a plea not for revolution but for social justice through better wages and working conditions for the dispossessed.

12. One way of approaching **Handout 23** might be to recall **Handout 13**, dealing with the evils of labeling. You might review from this handout the references to the novel in which Steinbeck defines "reds" and "bolsheviks." Elicit from students what they already know about the Russian Revolution and the leftist movement in American labor during the Depression. This could be a good opportunity to clarify with students the difference between ideology and practice (e.g., as before they discussed the American Dream as ideal and reality, they might see Communism as ideal and reality.) It is difficult for students to understand why so many people for so many decades would die for a cause they define simply as atheism. In comprehending the causes of the Russian Revolution, students may read stories about the Central American nations with a new understanding.

13. Students should be able to complete this as an out-of-class assignment.

Suggested Answers

1. *Remind students to seek answers that would make sense in the context of Steinbeck's quote. How were these men "revolutionaries"?*
   a) *Paine (1737–1809) pamphleteer, whose Common Sense (1776) demanded complete independence from England; returned to England and wrote The Rights of*

Man *(1791–2), a controversial reply to Edmund Burke's Reflections on the Revolution in France.*

b) *Marx (1818–1883) German political philosopher journalist, friend of Engels; together they wrote the Communist Manifesto (1848), with its famous exhortation, "Workers of the world unite." Marx took part in the revolutionary uprisings in the Rhineland in 1848 and after their failure settled (1849) in London for the rest of his life; called Father of Dialectical Materialism.*

c) *Jefferson (1743–1826) Third president of the United States; his political doctrines were based on those of Locke and Rousseau; his practice proved him to be one of the great liberal statespersons of history. Although with his followers he formed a new Republican party, in opposition to Hamilton and the Federalists, it was the ancestor of today's Democratic party. Jefferson was the chief writer of the Declaration of Independence.*

d) *Lenin (1870–1924) Chief theoretician of Marxism and creator of the Soviet state. Student of Marx who left Russia for England, he directed much of the first revolution from abroad, seized power in a second revolution, and was named premier from 1917 to 1924. In 1919 he established Communist International to foster world revolution. St Petersburg was named Leningrad five days after his death.*

2. *Those who own possessions and will not share from their plenty with the "have-nots" of the world often blame revolutionary thinkers for uprisings and ultimate social chaos. Steinbeck advises the "haves" to look to themselves for the reasons (the "causes") for revolution. The poor, in their hunger and concern for their families, often become violent when all other means fail.*

3. *The Wilsons and Joads pool their resources in ch. 13; Mae and the truck drivers share with the migrant father and sons in ch. 15.*

Assignment: Add to **Handouts 5** and **6.**

The Grapes of Wrath: An American Novel

"[Casey] went out in the wilderness to find his own soul, an 'he foun' he didn' have no soul that was his'n. Says he found he jus' got a little piece of a great big soul." (ch. 28)

In an article entitled "The Philosophical Joads," Frederic I. Carpenter writes: "Novels that have become classics do more than tell a story and describe characters; they offer insight into [people's] motives and point to the springs of action."[1] In short, a philosophy permeates them. Steinbeck's "philosophy" defies simple classification, but there is a uniquely Steinbeckian flavor to this American novel, gathering as it does, ideas from the poet Walt Whitman and philosophers Emerson, John Dewey, and William James.

From Emerson, he took the idea of an Oversoul. From Whitman, he borrowed the concept of democracy and the life-giving force of the masses. The Grapes of Wrath is, in fact, a distinctly American novel in its blending of the transcendental philosophy of Emerson and the pragmatism of John Dewey and William James. (It is no accident, for example, that Grampa's full name is William James Joad.) The Joads move from a rugged individualism and a concern for their family to concern for the human family.

1. Find definitions for these terms:
   a) Transcendentalism:

   b) Pragmatism:

2. The consequence of believing in an Oversoul is living by the truth that humankind is bound one to another with spiritual bonds. We become responsible for what happens to our neighbor and to society in general. Explain how this principle is exemplified in the actions of specific characters in this novel:

   Casy

[1]Frederic I. Carpenter College English, 2 (1941), 315.

Tom

Ma

Rose of Sharon

Wilsons

Wainwrights

3. In the "coal-black cave of vines," Tom tells Ma: "Then I'll be aroun' in the dark. I'll be ever' where—wherever you look. Wherever they's a fight so hungry people can eat, I'll be there. Wherever there's a cop beatin' up a guy, I'll be there" (ch. 28). What philosophy does Tom manifest with these words?

Naturalism? Maybe

John Steinbeck was a great lover and observer of the natural world. His close friendship with marine biologist Ed Ricketts and his themes of victimized lower classes led numerous critics to see John Steinbeck as a literary naturalist, one who applied principles of scientific determinism to his fiction. In realism, authors portray everyday life as objectively as possible. Naturalism, however, is a "form of extreme REALISM. . . . The naturalistic view of human beings is that of animals in the natural world, responding to environmental forces and internal stresses and drives, over none of which they have control and none of which they fully understand."[1]

Looking back over the novel, list five things you remember which might justify the term *naturalistic* to describe the novel:

1.

2.

3.

4.

5.

The most important of American literary naturalists—Theodore Dreiser, Frank Norris, Stephen Crane, Upton Sinclair, and Jack London—wrote stories that manifested Darwin's theory of "survival of the fittest." Beaten down by an inhuman system and bad luck, many of their characters end as suicides. While there are surely naturalistic features in *The Grapes of Wrath*, the characters of this novel are not mere fate-tossed animals who struggle towards "survival of the fittest." The characters are often beset by circumstances over which they have little control, but there are moments in the novel when, unlike animals, the characters make humane choices or decisions, when they overcome obstacles and go forward. List five such choices or decisions you can recall from the novel.

[1]C. Hugh Holman and William Harmon, *A Handbook to Literature*, 5th ed. (New York: Macmillan, 1986), 320.

Name _____

Date _____

1.

2.

3.

4.

5.

Marxism? No.

Here is the anlage of the thing you fear. This is the zygote. For here "I lost my land" is changed; a cell is split and from its splitting grows the thing you hate. "We lost *our* land . . . . This is the beginning-from 'I' to 'we'"

If you who own the things people must have could understand this, you might preserve yourselves. If you could separate causes from results, if you could know that Paine, Marx, Jefferson, Lenin, were results, not causes, you might survive. But that you cannot know. For the quality of owning freezes you forever into "I," and cuts you off forever from the "we." (ch. 14)

1. Who are:

  a) (Thomas) Paine:

  b) (Karl) Marx:

  c) (Thomas) Jefferson:

  d) (Vladimir Illych) Lenin:

2. What does this passage mean?

When *The Grapes of Wrath* was first published, critics rejected it for two major reasons: One group found the language offensive, and many libraries banned the book. A larger group, however, rejected the book on political grounds. Steinbeck's attack on the banks and land owners won him the label "Communist." The book was classified as propaganda, in the category of *Uncle Tom's Cabin* or Sinclair's *The Jungle*. Judged a proletarian novel because it dealt with the laboring classes, the novel was called Marxist by many readers in the Forties and Fifties.

Steinbeck, however, never saw Communism as an answer to the Joads' predicament. Rather, their only hope was a deep compassion for and a working together with one another. In chapter 14, for example, the narrator says, "The baby has a cold. Here, take this blanket. It's wool. It was my mother's blanket—take it for the baby."

3. What events in chapters 13 and 15 link this intercalary chapter on the necessity of sharing what one has, no matter how little?

Lesson 9

People/Machines/Animals: Unifying Motifs in *The Grapes of Wrath*

Objectives

- To help students to see how an author uses image patterns for unity, characterization, and explication of theme

- To enable students to see the novel as a unified whole

Notes to the Teacher

This lesson rewards the students' efforts in recording animal and machine imagery. Even if they discovered only a fraction of the many possibilities, the students will have collectively found enough examples to answer the questions in this lesson. The skills developed in this exercise will help them in reading novels for years to come.

Procedure

1. Students are already using many animal analogies in their everyday speech; e.g. quick as a rabbit, sly as a fox, etc. You might begin this lesson by soliciting from them all these expressions they can think of. Next, ask them how many cars they can think of named after animals (e.g. Cougar, Mustang, Pinto, Eagle, Lynx, Thunderbird). Discuss why these names might have been chosen.

2. If students have completed **Handout 6**, have them take it out and discuss the many references they found in the novel to animals and machines by chapter. You may, for example, want to list briefly on the board the characters described with animal imagery, as elicited from the students' handouts. (See suggested answers on pp. 11–13). Then see how many machine references they found and write major ones on the board (or overhead projector).

3. Distribute the first page of **Handout 24**. Using the textual references found by the students and the ones listed at the beginning of the handout, have

students, individually or in groups, answer questions 1–4. Go over the answers in a class discussion.

4. Distribute page 2 of the handout. Follow a similar procedure, using student references and the ones provided at the beginning of this handout. When you are sure students can finish the exercise on their own, assign them to complete it out of class to be returned in the next class period.

Assignment: Complete page 2.

Suggested Answers

1. *The people are reduced to animal level by the banks and owners; the people are close to nature, one with the land they farmed.*
2. *Tom's turtle, deserted cat in ch. 2, dogs left behind; the pet dog taken along is killed when run over by a passing car.*
3. *Some become wild; some are killed. The turtle begins a trek southwest.*
4. *Buzzards most often portend death. The rattlesnake is also a threat since it is a poisonous snake.*
5. *The truck continues to break down or have problems; its condition is, at best, precarious. Eventually it is completely stopped—as are the Joads.*
6. *Hardly; he knew that life would be easier if farmers had access to tractors. The problem was that they had no money, had to sell what little machinery they had for food, and couldn't compete with farmers who did own machines.*
7. *"If this tractor were ours it would be good, not mine but ours . . . . We could love that tractor then as we have loved this land when it was ours."*
8. *Answers will vary. Your preliminary discussion may have touched upon this topic, but if not, students will have to reflect from their own experience to answer the question.*

Putting the Pieces Together

Animals and machines are an important part of *The Grapes of Wrath* at both a literal and a symbolic level. They unify the novel, help us to understand characters, and point out major themes in the work.

In Lesson 2, you began to study the relationships among people, machines, and animals in this novel. Turtles, tractors, cats and cars appear in the early chapters, but animal similes abound throughout the book. Muley is "mean like a weasel" (ch. 6). Al acts like "a dunghill rooster" (ch. 28). The roads to California are full of migrants who "scuttled" and "clustered like bugs" (ch. 17); the strikers are driven "like pigs" (ch. 26). Tom lives "like a rabbit" (ch. 28) on the run. Ma says, "All we got is the family unbroke. Like a bunch of cows, when the lobos are ranging, stick all together" (ch. 16).

1. Why might Steinbeck have used so many references to animals in describing his characters?

2. Another way that Steinbeck uses animal imagery in the novel is through the inclusion of pets early in the story. How many pets (or animals destined to become pets) do you remember?

3. What happened to these animals?

4. Animals are sometimes used as omens in the story. What might the buzzard in ch. 16 signify? Or the rattlesnake Tom kills as they prepare to enter California?

Steinbeck's use of machine imagery is more complex in the novel. Tractors "tear in and shove the croppers out" (ch. 2), but the truck becomes their "new hearth, the living center of the family" (ch. 10). Used-car lots appear throughout the novel, their unscrupulous salesmen cheating the desperate migrants who cannot walk to California. Mechanization has driven out the team and wagon farmers of Oklahoma. In the novel, it is not machines that are evil, but the system that allows only the wealthy to own the tractors.

5. In what ways does the condition of the Joads' truck reflect their sad situation?

When Steinbeck combines the machine and animal imagery, we get the "monster" image: The bank-owned tractors are "snubnosed monsters, raising the dust and sticking their snouts into it" (ch. 5). The driver becomes "part of the monster, a robot in the seat" (ch. 5). When the hungry men are building the dam in ch. 30, "they worked jerkily, like machines."

6. Do you think Steinbeck is saying that America should have abandoned machines and technology to preserve the family-owned farms with a team of horses?

7. From all you have studied of these image patterns, what seems to be Steinbeck's attitude towards the machine? (See ch. 14, par. 2)

8. Is living in a technological world still problematic for us? Explain your answer.

Lesson 10

"The Education of the Heart": A Way of Understanding the Novel as a Whole

Objectives

- To help students to see the linkage between the novel's beginning and its end
- To provide an opportunity for students to examine the values inherent in Steinbeck's novel
- To allow students to project the Joads' future in light of what they know from the story

Notes to the Teacher

This final lesson is designed to pull together the entire unit by exploring a central motif in the novel: the Joads' "education of the heart." If students have been completing successive handouts in this unit, this lesson should provide a way of understanding the novel as a whole. In addition, the final handout, with its inherent question, "What next?" allows students to discuss the future of the Joads and their neighbors in pre-World War II California, once again linking history with literature.

Procedure

1. Have students take out page 2 of **Handout 24** to use as a basis for class discussion.

2. Introduce the final lesson by showing students a few of the connecting links between the novel's beginning and end; e.g. read aloud the passage in ch. 1: "After a while the faces of the watching men lost their bemused perplexity and became hard and angry and resistant. Then the women knew that they were safe and that there was no break. . . . Women and children knew deep in themselves that no misfortune was too great to bear if their men were whole." And in ch. 29: "The women watched the men, watched to see whether the break had come at last. The women stood silently and watched. And where a number of men gathered together, the fear went from their faces, and anger took its place.

And the women sighed with relief, for they knew it was all right-the break had not come; and the break would never come as long as fear could turn to wrath."

Discuss the similarities; then contrast the Okies' praying for an end to the drought (ch. 2), followed by chapters 29 and 30's downpour and flood. Show that in both cases, nature was cruel to the migrants and that chapter 29 is a premonition of the bleakness of the last chapter.

3. Having discussed the grim reality facing the novel's main characters, open discussion to Rose of Sharon's action and see if any students see in this symbolic offering a "hope for humanity."

4. Distribute **Handout 25** and use as a discussion guide after students have read its contents.

5. Allow students to work out answers to questions 1 and 2 in their small groups.

6. Discuss their answers.

   Suggested Answers

   1. *Weedpatch experience; the flood and dam building; Tom's having to hide out; kindness shown them by others*

   2. *Ma—dissolution of family in spite of best efforts; death of Rose of Sharon's child*
      Pa finally springs into action to build dam after the flood
      Tom—his time in hiding (like Casy's in prison) provides time to think; decides to take up Casy's cause and help workers to organize
      Al—gives up "tom-cattin'," settles down to marry Agnes and begin his own family
      Ruthie—gives flower (with some remorse) to Winfield at the novel's end Uncle John—sends stillborn as prophetic messenger downstream

Casy—risks and finally gives up his life for the cause of the mistreated workers

7. Distribute **Handout 26** and have students discuss the "future" for the Joads. This handout provides an opportunity to re-emphasize the humane ending of the novel (disputed by many critics) and to link the novel once more to actual historical events.

Suggested Answers

1. *His purpose was to have the readers see that even when the Joads had nothing, life and suffering had taught them to share what little they had; in this case, Rose of Sharon's breast milk*

2. *Answers will vary, but you may expect suggestions that some Joads will be dead, Tom will be in prison or killed, Al and Aggie will be married, and he'll have a job in the garage, etc.*

3. *The war took some of the men in the draft. Aircraft plants employed men and women, creating a need for an employment of the destitute migrants. Most stayed in California, and the war, ironically, brought an end to their desperation.*

4. *Yes, the quotation at the beginning of the handout confirms this.*

Assignment: Turn in **Handout 5**, which has received continuous attention throughout this unit, for evaluation and credit.

Name _____

Date _____

That Controversial Ending

> Ma's eyes passed Rose of Sharon's eyes, and then came back to them. And the two women looked deep into each other. The girl's breath came short and gasping.
>
> She said, "Yes."
>
> Ma smiled. "I knowed you would. I knowed!" (ch. 30)

Nothing in *The Grapes of Wrath* so outraged its first readers as the scene in chapter 30 where Rose of Sharon offers her breast to save the dying man from starvation. Clifton Fadiman in *The New Yorker* wrote that "the ending is the tawdriest kind of fake symbolism."[1] Many critics would agree with him, but if we examine the novel closely we find that the ending is "right." Rose of Sharon, who so often in the early chapters is a whining, selfish, immature girl, grows into a woman like her mother, who cares for others first, no matter the cost. In fact, at the novel's end, we find that each of the major characters has changed. In Warren French's term, each has received an "education of the heart," resulting "in a change from the family's jealously regarding itself as an isolated and self-important clan to its envisioning itself as part of one vast human family."[2] Most begin, like Tom, "jus' puttin' one foot in front a the other" (ch. 16). Uncle John lives in the past, harboring guilt over his wife's death. Al lives for girls and cars. Pa is so broken at the loss of his farm that for much of the novel he allows all decisions to be made by Ma. Ma at the novel's beginning has only one passion: to keep the "fambly" together. Ruthie torments her brother and exhibits childish ways until almost the end of the book. Even Casy, when the novel opens, is adrift. He's sure there's something to be learned in the midst of all the suffering, but until he goes to prison, even he lacks real conviction or directed action.

The critical reader sees a change coming that is more than a restlessness in the land. The main characters by chapter 30 have all undergone an education. The suffering has changed them, has redeemed them. We've already looked at the point at which Rose of Sharon proves she has changed. In the space below, identify points in the novel or actions which exhibit change in the other characters:

1. Can you identify events in the novel which help to change the hearts of the Joads?

---

[1]Warren French, "From Naturalism to the Drama of Consciousness—The Education of the Heart in *The Grapes of Wrath*," in *Twentieth Century Interpretations of The Grapes of Wrath*, ed. Robert Con Davis (Englewood Cliffs, NJ: Prentice Hall, 1982), 25.

[2]*Ibid.*, 26.

Name _____

Date _____

2. Can you identify events in the lives of the following characters where they show that they have changed?

Ma

Pa

Tom

Al

Ruthie

Uncle John

Casy

Name _____

Date _____

Chapter 31: The Future of the Joads

"One other thing—I am not writing a satisfying story. I've done my damndest to rip a reader's nerves to rags, I don't want him [or her] satisfied" (*Letters*, p. 178)

Even if we believe that the characters experience a change of heart at the novel's end, their future is still rather bleak. Casy's dead. Tom runs the same risk by taking up his cause. Al has stayed behind in the flooded boxcar with Aggie and the Wainrights—but they have no work or food. Ma and Pa Joad, Uncle John, Rose of Sharon, Ruthie and Winfield take shelter in a barn, where they come across the dying man and his son. They have no food, no money, no car, no hope of immediate employment. And the rains continue.

1. Why does Steinbeck end the novel with Rose of Sharon's feeding the dying man and not emphasize their plight?

2. If you had a crystal ball and could see into the future, what would your "chapter 31" contain?

3. What *did* happen to the Joads (and their neighbors) in California after 1939?

4. Could Steinbeck have wanted his readers to be moved to write an alternative ending, as did Dickens in "A Christmas Carol"? If yes, what would it be?

Supplementary Material
A Word About the Film

Because the novel's film version is easily available for purchase or rental, teachers who opt to show the film in class should be aware of some facts about the production. The picture lost out to *Rebecca* for the Best Picture Award of 1940, but John Ford and Jane Darwell both won as Best Director and Actress, respectively. For its time, the realism and political tenor of the film were revolutionary.

Viewed five decades later, however, the film seems more a period piece than the critical success of an earlier era. The black-and-white "documentary" quality of the film remains. Some of the scenes linger in the memory, especially the overloaded truck, the Oklahoma house-demolishing, and the farewell of Ma and Tom. Censorship barred almost all of the objectional language from the film, and the acting, in general, far surpassed much of what we see today on evening television.

But the real problem with the film version of Steinbeck's novel is that at many levels it isn't the same story—or, rather, it's another version of the same story. The Wilsons, the Wainwrights, the religious fanatics are conspicuously absent. There is not only no symbolic turtle, there are almost no animals (or animal references) at all. Uncle John, Ruthie, and Winfield are so nondescript as characters that the story would not have lost anything by their not being a part of the film. Ma's passion to keep her family together (which does remain in the film) is seriously undercut when Noah simply vanishes from the picture—and not a soul even wonders where he is!

The episode at Weedpatch, displaced from the novel version, is part of the upbeat ending of the film. Tom does not hide in a cave. Ruthie doesn't tell anyone that her brother killed two men. In fact, Rose of Sharon is still looking forward to the birth of a new generation at the picture's end. The sun's shining (no rain, no flood), and Ma gives her speech of chapter 20 that the family will go on forever because "We're the people."

In short, students who saw this film and did not read the novel could not complete most of the handouts. The intercalary structure of the book is transfigured in the film so that Muley's role is greatly enlarged. (He becomes some of the "anonymous" characters in the interchapters.) In similar fashion, the Joads take on some of the anonymous roles. Pa tries to buy the ten-cent loaf of bread from Mae, and Ruthie and Winfield get the "penny candy."

The film is an American movie classic. None of these comments are designed to discourage you from viewing the film. It's just such a radical shift in emphasis, tone, story line, and characterization that no teacher should make the assumption that the film would help students to understand the novel better. The best classroom use of the film is probably to show it after the novel has been studied and have students write an essay indicating whether they preferred the novel or film. This is an excellent opportunity for evaluating how well students grasped the meaning of Steinbeck's novel.

Two critical reviews which may be of further pre-viewing help to you are "*The Grapes of Wrath*" in *Cinema: The Novel Into Film* (part of the Magill Surveys), pp. 206-8, and the classic film review by George Bluestone, "*The Grapes of Wrath*," which originally appeared in his *From Novels Into Film*, but can be found in *Twentieth Century Interpretations of The Grapes of Wrath*, pp. 79-99. See the bibliography at the end of this unit for complete bibliographical information.

Supplementary Materials

Essay Questions

1. Is Steinbeck fair to the California owners? Does he present them all as heartless, cruel, and exploitative of the poor? Can you find any people in the novel who try to be kind to the migrants who arrive penniless in California?

2. How are the turtle (in the opening chapters) and the Joads alike? Is there significance in the turtle's getting across the road against all odds and heading southwest, dropping seeds as it moves along?

3. Give examples of how Steinbeck presents religion in this novel. Does he condemn organized religion throughout the novel in favor of a sort of personal mysticism, or does he make a distinction between genuine religious expression and self-righteous, hypocritical religious people?

4. Why is it fitting that Grampa and Grandma never make it to California?

5. In what ways does this novel transcend the critical issues of the Thirties and the Depression and speak to us in our day? Are there issues that are the same for us? Explain.

6. Why do Casy and Tom get involved in the strikes and helping people they don't even know? Wouldn't it have been smarter to continue minding their own business and taking care of themselves and their family? Can you think of others today who take up causes from which they could just as easily have walked away?

7. One of Steinbeck's major themes in this novel is that America was undergoing great change during this period. Is America still undergoing great change, or have we reached a point where change is in much smaller things? Give examples to support either position.

Supplementary Materials
Vocabulary Words

Note to Teacher

Below are some of the words that may be troublesome to students. You may put the words on the board as you cover the chapters or point them out in class discussion. Students may put the definitions in their notebooks for extra credit, adding any other words they may find unfamiliar.

Chapter		Chapter	
1	chambray	13	forties [side by side]
2	anlage	14	zygote
4	molting	15	mica
	swale		quoit
6	burble	16	babbitt lobos
8	lecherous	18	heliograph
	Mother Hubbard	20	Hooverville
	Hatfield and McCoy blood		blacklist
9	[smells] rank	21	rachitic
10	smoker of snipes		pustules
	hoyden		pellagra
	jake	22	frawny
	fatuously	24	vagrant
	stereopticon		two-bit [man]
	squidged	28	effluvium
	splayed	29	mastoids
	titular		
	carborundum stone		
	tarpaulin		
12	tappets		
	zenith		
	truculence		

Supplementary Material

Final Test

I. Match the following quotations in Column A with the speakers from Column B. (5 pts. each)

A

1. (   ) "Time was when a man said what we'd do. Seems like a woman is tellin' now. Seems like it's purty near time to get out a stick."

2. (   ) "We're the people—we go on."

3. (   ) "Then I'll be aroun' in the dark. I'll be ever'where wherever you look. Wherever they's a fight so hungry people can eat, I'll be there."

4. (   ) "You can't get no loaf a bread for a dime. We only got fifteen-cent loaves."

5. (   ) "They stoled my Cracker Jack! That big son-of-a bitch of a girl, she belted me."

6. (   ) "I ain't feelin' good. Connie shouldn' of left me."

7. (   ) "You go right on along. Me—I'm stayin.' I give her a goin' over all night mos'ly. This here's my country. I b'long here. . . . This country ain't no good, but it's my country."

8. (   ) "All that lives is holy."

9. (   ) "They ain't nothin' I love like the guts of a en-gine."

10. ( ) "Go down an' tell 'em. Go down in the street an' rot an' tell 'em that way. That's the way you can talk. Don't even know if you was a boy or a girl."

B

1. Ruthie
2. Ma Joad
3. Grampa
4. Tom Joad
5. Uncle John
6. Rose of Sharon
7. Pa Joad
8. Al Joad
9. Casy
10. Mae

II. Fill in the Blanks. (5 pts. each):

1. Jim Casy was a _____ before the novel begins, and the Joads still think of him as one.

2. _____ is aptly named in the beginning of the novel. He de-scribes himself as a graveyard ghost.

3. _____ dies in Ma Joad's arms as they drive across the desert.

4. _____ is the guilt-ridden "black sheep" of the Joad family, who feels responsible for his young wife's death from a ruptured appendix.

5. _____ provides a blanket to bury Grampa in, and she and her husband join forces with the Joads by adding their car to the Joad's truck.

III. Answer the following question in a short essay for 25 pts.

What is the purpose of the intercalary chapters in Steinbeck's novel? Can you recall any links between the novel's chapters?

Supplementary Materials
Answers to Final Test

Part One:

1. 7		6. 6		
2. 2		7. 3		
3. 4		8. 9		
4. 10		9. 8		
5. 1		10. 5		

Part Two:

1. preacher
2. Muley Graves
3. Granma
4. Uncle John
5. Sairy Wilson

Part Three: Answers will vary. See Lesson 2, **Handout 5** for examples.

Bibliography

Astro, Richard, and Tetsumaro Hayashi, eds. *Steinbeck: The Man and His Work.* Corvallis: Oregon State University Press, 1971.

Carpenter, Frederic I. "The Philosophical Joads." *College English,* 2 (1941): 315.

Davis, Robert Con, ed. *Twentieth Century Interpretations* of THE GRAPES OF WRATH. Englewood Cliffs, N.J.: Prentice-Hall, 1982.

Davis, Robert Murray, ed. *Steinbeck: A Collection of Critical Essays.* Englewood Cliffs, N.J.: Prentice-Hall, 1972.

Donohue, Agnes Mc Neill, ed. *A Casebook on* THE GRAPES OF WRATH. New York: Crowell, 1968.

Fontenrose, Joseph. *John Steinbeck: An Introduction and Interpretation.* New York: Holt, Rinehart, and Winston, 1963.

French, Warren. *A Companion to* THE GRAPES OF WRATH. New York: Viking Press, 1963.

————. *John Steinbeck.* New York: Twayne, 1961.

Hayashi, Tetsumaro, ed. *A Study Guide to Steinbeck: A Handbook to His Major Works.* Metuchen, N.J.: Scarecrow Press, 1974.

Holman, C. Hugh and William Harmon. *A Handbook to Literature.* 5th ed. New York: Macmillan, 1986.

Levant, Howard. *The Novels of John Steinbeck: A Critical Study.* Columbia: University of Maryland Press, 1974.

Lisca, Peter. *The Wide World of John Steinbeck.* New Brunswick, N.J.: Rutgers University Press, 1958.

Magill, Frank N., ed. *Cinema: The Novel Into Film.* Pasadena: Salem Press, 1980.

Owens, Louis. *John Steinbeck's Re-Vision of America.* Athens, Ga.: University of Georgia, 1985.

Steinbeck, Elaine, and Robert Wallsten, eds. *Steinbeck: A Life in Letters.* New York: Viking Press, 1975.

Steinbeck, John. *The Grapes of Wrath.* New York: Penguin Books, 1981. *Time,* 2 January 1989: 24-73.

Timmerman, John S. *John Steinbeck's Fiction: The Aesthetics of the Road Taken.* Norman, Okla.: University of Oklahoma Press, 1986.

Acknowledgments

For permission to reprint all works in this volume by each of the following authors, grateful acknowledgment is made to the holders of copyright, publishers, or representatives named below.

Introduction: Lesson 5, Handout 14; Lesson 10, Handout 26

Excerpts from *Steinbeck: A Life in Letters*, ed. Elaine Steinbeck and Robert Wallsten, 1975. Published by Viking-Penguin, Inc., New York, NY.

Excerpts from *The Grapes of Wrath* by John Steinbeck, 1981. Published by Penguin Books, Inc., New York, NY.

Novel/Drama Series

Novel

*Absolutely Normal Chaos/
    Chasing Redbird,* Creech
Across Five Aprils, Hunt
Adam of the Road, Gray/
    Catherine, Called Birdy, Cushman
The Adventures of Huckleberry Finn, Twain
The Adventures of Tom Sawyer, Twain
The Age of Innocence, Wharton
*Alice's Adventures in Wonderland/
    Through the Looking-Glass,* Carroll
All Creatures Great and Small, Herriot
All Quiet on the Western Front, Remarque
All the King's Men, Warren
All the Pretty Horses, McCarthy
Among the Hidden/Among the Impostors,
    Haddix
Animal Farm, Orwell/
    The Book of the Dun Cow, Wangerin Jr.
Anna Karenina, Tolstoy
Anne Frank: The Diary of a Young Girl, Frank
Anne of Green Gables, Montgomery
April Morning, Fast
As I Lay Dying, Faulkner
The Assistant/The Fixer, Malamud
The Autobiography of Miss Jane Pittman,
    Gaines
The Awakening, Chopin/
    Madame Bovary, Flaubert
Babbitt, Lewis
The Bean Trees/Pigs in Heaven, Kingsolver
Belle Prater's Boy, White/
    My Louisiana Sky, Holt
Beowulf/Grendel, Gardner
Billy Budd/Moby Dick, Melville
Black Boy, Wright
Black Elk Speaks, Neihardt
Blessings, Quindlen
Bless Me, Ultima, Anaya
Brave New World, Huxley
Brideshead Revisited, Waugh
The Bridge of San Luis Rey, Wilder
The Brothers Karamazov, Dostoevsky
Bud, Not Buddy, Curtis/*Sounder,* Armstrong
Burning Up, Cooney/*The Watcher,* Howe
The Call of the Wild/White Fang, London
The Canterbury Tales, Chaucer
Catch–22, Heller
The Catcher in the Rye, Salinger
The Cay/Timothy of the Cay, Taylor
Celebration!/ Counterfeit Legacy, Moser
Ceremony, Silko
Charlotte's Web, White/
    The Secret Garden, Burnett
Charming Billy/At Weddings and Wakes,
    McDermott
The Chosen, Potok
The Christmas Box, Evans/
    A Christmas Carol, Dickens
Chronicles of Narnia, Lewis

Cold Mountain, Frazier
Cold Sassy Tree, Burns
*The Color of Water: A Black Man's Tribute to
    His White Mother,* McBride
*A Connecticut Yankee in King Arthur's
    Court,* Twain
The Count of Monte Cristo, Dumas
Crime and Punishment, Dostoevsky
Cry, the Beloved Country, Paton
The Crystal Cave, Stewart
Dandelion Wine, Bradbury
David Copperfield, Dickens
Davita's Harp, Potok
A Day No Pigs Would Die, Peck
Death Comes for the Archbishop, Cather
December Stillness, Hahn/
    Izzy, Willy-Nilly, Voigt
Demian, Hesse/
    The Illustrated Man, Bradbury
Dinner at the Homesick Restaurant, Tyler
The Divine Comedy, Dante
The Dollmaker, Arnow
Don Quixote, Cervantes
Dr. Zhivago, Pasternak
Dubliners, Joyce
East of Eden, Steinbeck
The Egypt Game, Snyder/
    The Bronze Bow, Speare
Ellen Foster/A Virtuous Woman, Gibbons
Emma, Austen
Ender's Game, Card
Fahrenheit 451, Bradbury
Far North, Hobbs/*Shipwreck at the Bottom
    of the World,* Armstrong
A Farewell to Arms, Hemingway
Farewell to Manzanar, Houston and Hous-
    ton/*Black Like Me,* Griffin
Forbidden City, Bell/*The Ear, the Eye, and
    the Arm,* Farmer
Frankenstein, Shelley
*Fried Green Tomatoes/Welcome to the
    World, Baby Girl!,* Flagg
*From the Mixed-up Files of Mrs. Basil E.
    Frankweiler,* Konigsburg/
    The Westing Game, Raskin
A Gathering of Flowers, Thomas, ed.
The Ghost Walker/The Dream Stalker, Coel
The Giver, Lowry
The Good Earth, Buck
The Grapes of Wrath, Steinbeck
Great Expectations, Dickens
The Great Gatsby, Fitzgerald
Gulliver's Travels, Swift
The Gypsy Game, Snyder/
    The Trumpeter of Krakow, Kelly
Habibi, Nye/*Seven Daughters and Seven
    Sons,* Cohen and Lovejoy
Hard Times, Dickens
Hatchet, Paulsen/
    Robinson Crusoe, Defoe
Having Our Say, Delany, Delany, and Hearth/
    A Gathering of Old Men, Gaines
The Heart Is a Lonely Hunter, McCullers
Heart of Darkness, Conrad
Hiroshima, Hersey/*On the Beach,* Shute
The Hobbit, Tolkien

Holes, Sachar/*Out of the Dust,* Hesse
Homecoming/Dicey's Song, Voigt
The Hound of the Baskervilles, Doyle
The House on Mango Street, Cisneros
The House of the Spirits, Allende
Howards End, Forster
*The Human Comedy/
    My Name Is Aram,* Saroyan
I Know Why the Caged Bird Sings, Angelou
The Iliad, Homer
Incident at Hawk's Hill, Eckert/
    Where the Red Fern Grows, Rawls
In the Time of the Butterflies, Alvarez
Into Thin Air, Krakauer
Invisible Man, Ellison
Jane Eyre, Brontë
Johnny Tremain, Forbes
Journey of the Sparrows, Buss and Cubias/
    The Honorable Prison, de Jenkins
The Joy Luck Club, Tan
Jubal Sackett/The Walking Drum, L'Amour
Jude the Obscure, Hardy
Julie of the Wolves, George/
    Island of the Blue Dolphins, O'Dell
The Jungle, Sinclair
The Killer Angels, Shaara
The Kite Runner, Hosseini
Le Morte D'Arthur, Malory
The Learning Tree, Parks
Les Miserables, Hugo
A Lesson before Dying, Gaines/
    The Green Mile, King
*Light in August/*Faulkner
*The Light in the Forest/
    A Country of Strangers,* Richter
*Little House in the Big Woods/
    Little House on the Prairie,* Wilder
The Little Prince, Saint-Exupéry
Little Women, Alcott
Lonesome Dove, McMurtry
*A Long Way from Chicago/
    A Year Down Yonder,* Peck
Looking Backward, Bellamy
Lord of the Flies, Golding
The Lord of the Rings, Tolkien
The Lovely Bones, Sebold
The Martian Chronicles, Bradbury
The Member of the Wedding, McCullers/
    A Christmas Memory, Capote
The Metamorphosis, Kafka/
    The Death of Ivan Ilyich, Tolstoy
Missing May, Rylant/
    The Summer of the Swans, Byars
The Moviegoer, Percy/
    Father Melancholy's Daughter, Godwin
Mrs. Mike, Freedman/
    I Heard the Owl Call My Name, Craven
*Murder on the Orient Express/
    And Then There Were None,* Christie
My Antonia, Cather
Narrative of the Life of Frederick Douglass,
    Douglass
Native Son, Wright
The Natural, Malamud/
    Shoeless Joe, Kinsella
Nectar in a Sieve, Markandaya/
    The Woman Warrior, Kingston

Night, Wiesel

Nightjohn/Soldier's Heart, Paulsen

A Night to Remember, Lord/*Streams to the River, River to the Sea*, O'Dell

1984, Orwell

Number the Stars, Lowry/*Friedrich*, Richter

Obasan, Kogawa

The Odyssey, Homer

The Old Man and the Sea, Hemingway/*Ethan Frome*, Wharton

Oliver Twist, Dickens

The Once and Future King, White

One Day in the Life of Ivan Denisovich, Solzhenitsyn/*Man's Search for Meaning*, Frankl

One Hundred Years of Solitude, García Márquez

O Pioneers!, Cather/*The Country of the Pointed Firs*, Jewett

Ordinary People, Guest/*The Tin Can Tree*, Tyler

The Outsiders, Hinton/*Durango Street*, Bonham

Paradise Lost, Milton

A Passage to India/Forster

A Patchwork Planet, Tyler

The Pearl/Of Mice and Men, Steinbeck

The Picture of Dorian Gray, Wilde/*Dr. Jekyll and Mr. Hyde*, Stevenson

The Pigman/The Pigman's Legacy, Zindel

The Poisonwood Bible, Kingsolver

The Ponder Heart/One Writer's Beginnings, Welty

A Portrait of the Artist as a Young Man, Joyce

The Portrait of a Lady, James

The Power and the Glory, Greene

A Prayer for Owen Meany, Irving

Pride and Prejudice, Austen

The Prince, Machiavelli/*Utopia*, More

The Prince and the Pauper, Twain

The Princess Bride, Goldman

Profiles in Courage, Kennedy

Pudd'nhead Wilson, Twain

Rebecca, du Maurier

The Red Badge of Courage, Crane

Red Scarf Girl, Jiang/*Chinese Cinderella*, Mah

Red Sky at Morning, Bradford

The Return of the Native, Hardy

A River Runs Through It, Maclean

Roll of Thunder, Hear My Cry/Let the Circle Be Unbroken, Taylor

Saint Maybe, Tyler

Sarum, Rutherfurd

The Scarlet Letter, Hawthorne

The Scarlet Pimpernel, Orczy

The Secret Life of Bees, Kidd

Sense and Sensibility, Austen

A Separate Peace, Knowles

Shabanu: Daughter of the Wind/Haveli, Staples

Shane, Schaefer/*The Ox-Bow Incident*, Van Tilburg Clark

The Shipping News, Proulx

Siddhartha, Hesse

The Sign of the Chrysanthemum/The Master Puppeteer, Paterson

The Signet Classic Book of Southern Short Stories, Abbott and Koppelman, eds.

Silas Marner, Eliot/*The Elephant Man*, Sparks

Sir Gawain and the Green Knight/Ivanhoe, Sir Walter Scott

Slaughterhouse-Five, Vonnegut

The Slave Dancer, Fox/*I, Juan de Pareja*, De Treviño

Snow Falling on Cedars, Guterson

Something Wicked This Way Comes, Bradbury

Song of Solomon, Morrison

The Song of the Lark, Cather

The Sound and the Fury, Faulkner

Spoon River Anthology, Masters

A Stranger Is Watching/I'll Be Seeing You, Higgins Clark

The Stranger/The Plague, Camus

Summer of My German Soldier, Greene/*Waiting for the Rain*, Gordon

Survival in Auschwitz, Levi

A Tale of Two Cities, Dickens

Talking God/A Thief of Time, Hillerman

Tangerine, Bloor/*Bleachers*, Grisham

Tara Road/The Return Journey, Binchy

Tess of the D'Urbervilles, Hardy

Their Eyes Were Watching God, Hurston

Things Fall Apart/No Longer at Ease, Achebe

The Things They Carried, O'Brien

Till We Have Faces, Lewis

To Kill a Mockingbird, Lee

To the Lighthouse, Woolf

Travels with Charley, Steinbeck

Treasure Island, Stevenson

A Tree Grows in Brooklyn, Smith

Tuck Everlasting, Babbitt/*Bridge to Terabithia*, Paterson

Tuesdays with Morrie, Albom

The Turn of the Screw/Daisy Miller, James

Uncle Tom's Cabin, Stowe

The Unvanquished, Faulkner

Walden, Thoreau/*A Different Drummer*, Kelley

Walk Two Moons, Creech

Walkabout, Marshall

Watership Down, Adams

The Watsons Go to Birmingham—1963, Curtis/*The View from Saturday*, Konigsburg

The Way to Rainy Mountain, Momaday/*The Whale Rider*, Ihimaera

When I Was Puerto Rican, Santiago

When the Legends Die, Borland

Where the Lilies Bloom, Cleaver/*No Promises in the Wind*, Hunt

The White Mountains, Christopher/*The True Confessions of Charlotte Doyle*, Avi

The Wild Birds: Six Stories of the Port William Membership, Berry

Winesburg, Ohio, Anderson

Wise Blood/O'Connor

The Witch of Blackbird Pond, Speare/*My Brother Sam Is Dead*, Collier and Collier

A Wrinkle in Time, L'Engle/*The Lion, the Witch and the Wardrobe*, Lewis

Wuthering Heights, Brontë

The Yearling, Rawlings/*The Red Pony*, Steinbeck

Year of Impossible Goodbyes, Choi/*So Far from the Bamboo Grove*, Watkins

Zlata's Diary, Filipovic/*The Lottery Rose*, Hunt

Drama

All My Sons, Miller

Antigone, Sophocles

Arms and the Man/Saint Joan, Shaw

The Crucible, Miller

Cyrano de Bergerac, Rostand

Death of a Salesman, Miller

A Doll's House/Hedda Gabler, Ibsen

Equus, Shaffer

The Glass Menagerie, Williams

The Importance of Being Earnest, Wilde

Inherit the Wind, Lawrence and Lee

Long Day's Journey into Night, O'Neill

Major Barbara/Mrs. Warren's Profession, Shaw

A Man for All Seasons, Bolt

"MASTER HAROLD" . . . *and the boys*, Fugard/*Fences*, Wilson

Medea, Euripides/*The Lion in Winter*, Goldman

The Miracle Worker, Gibson

Murder in the Cathedral, Eliot/*Galileo*, Brecht

The Night Thoreau Spent in Jail, Lawrence and Lee

Oedipus the King, Sophocles

The Oresteia/Aeschylus

Our Town, Wilder

The Piano Lesson, Wilson

The Playboy of the Western World/Riders to the Sea, Synge

Pygmalion, Shaw

A Raisin in the Sun, Hansberry

1776, Stone and Edwards

She Stoops to Conquer, Goldsmith/*The Matchmaker*, Wilder

A Streetcar Named Desire, Williams

Tartuffe, Molière

Three Comedies of American Family Life: I Remember Mama, van Druten/*Life with Father*, Lindsay and Crouse/*You Can't Take It with You*, Hart and Kaufman

The Trip to Bountiful, Foote/*Wit*, Edson

Waiting for Godot, Beckett/*Rosencrantz and Guildenstern Are Dead*, Stoppard

Shakespeare

As You Like It

Hamlet

Henry IV, Part I

Henry V

Julius Caesar

King Lear

Macbeth

The Merchant of Venice

A Midsummer Night's Dream

Much Ado about Nothing

Othello

Richard III

Romeo and Juliet

The Taming of the Shrew

The Tempest

Twelfth Night

The Center for Learning

The Publisher

All instructional materials identified by the TAP® (Teachers/Authors/Publishers) trademark are developed by a national network of 460 teacher-authors, whose collective educational experience distinguishes the publishing objective of The Center for Learning, a nonprofit educational corporation founded in 1970.

Concentrating on values-related disciplines, the Center publishes humanities and religion curriculum units for use in public and private schools and other educational settings. Approximately 600 language arts, social studies, novel/drama, life issues, and faith publications are available.

Publications are regularly evaluated and updated to meet the changing and diverse needs of teachers and students. Teachers may offer suggestions for development of new publications or revisions of existing titles by contacting

The Center for Learning
Administration/Creative Development
P.O. Box 417, Evergreen Road
Villa Maria, PA 16155
(800) 767-9090 • FAX (724) 964-1802

The Center for Learning
Editorial/Prepress
24600 Detroit Road, Suite 201
Westlake, OH 44145
(440) 250-9341 • FAX (440) 250-9715

For a free catalog containing order and price information and a descriptive listing of titles, contact

The Center for Learning
Customer Service
P.O. Box 910, Evergreen Road
Villa Maria, PA 16155
(724) 964-8083 • (800) 767-9090
FAX (888) 767-8080
http://www.centerforlearning.org